Thomas Rawson Birks

The Difficulties of Belief

In connexion with the creation and the fall, redemption and judgement. Second

Edition

Thomas Rawson Birks

The Difficulties of Belief
In connexion with the creation and the fall, redemption and judgement. Second Edition

ISBN/EAN: 9783337815738

Printed in Europe, USA, Canada, Australia, Japan

Cover: Foto ©Andreas Hilbeck / pixelio.de

More available books at **www.hansebooks.com**

THE

DIFFICULTIES OF BELIEF,

IN CONNEXION WITH

THE CREATION AND THE FALL,
REDEMPTION AND JUDGMENT.

THE

DIFFICULTIES OF BELIEF,

IN CONNEXION WITH

THE CREATION AND THE FALL.
REDEMPTION AND JUDGMENT.

BY

THOMAS RAWSON BIRKS, M.A.
PROFESSOR OF MORAL PHILOSOPHY AND THEOLOGY,
AND
VICAR OF HOLY TRINITY, CAMBRIDGE.

SECOND EDITION, ENLARGED.

London:
MACMILLAN AND CO.
1876.

Cambridge:

PRINTED BY C. J. CLAY, M.A.,

AT THE UNIVERSITY PRESS.

CONTENTS.

PREFACE TO THE FIRST EDITION.

THE object of the following Essay is to remove some of those difficulties which have often haunted thoughtful and inquiring minds, when they reflect on the deeper truths and more solemn aspects of religion, both natural and revealed. As it is to readers of this class alone that it is addressed, the work should be read with reference to its own object. There are some, perhaps, whose childlike faith is content to follow the plainer lessons of natural conscience and of Christian revelation, without being ever troubled by the dark shadows that lie around them. The aim of these pages is not to awaken the sense of difficulty in their minds, but to relieve the depth of these shadows, where they have been felt in their chilling and depressing power. In the hope that the views here partly unfolded, and which are not hastily entertained, may be to some weary spirits like a streak of morning light upon the distant mountains, when the gloom of night is passing away, they are committed to the blessing of the true Fountain of all wisdom.

KELSHALL, *Nov.* 1855.

PREFACE TO THE SECOND EDITION.

In the "Ways of God", published in October 1863, the line of thought in the first edition of this work was continued, and applied to the difficulties in Providence and Redemption. The subjects there treated were the long continuance of moral evil, the perils of human probation, the infrequency of miracles, the vanity of human life, the moral anomalies of providence, the Incarnation, the Atonement, Regeneration, Predestination, and the Supposed Failure of Christianity. In the preface I was able to mention, with deep thankfulness, that many testimonies had reached me, both from dear and intimate friends, some of them since removed by death, and from strangers personally unknown, of help and comfort received from the former work, in removing dark clouds, which had burdened their spirits, and obscured their vision of the Divine goodness. Some of these were from missionaries, both in the north and south of India, who had found help from it in their conflict with the dark fatalism, by which Mohammedans and Buddhists are alike fenced, as with a buckler, from the appeals of the Gospel. Many other testimonies of the same kind have reached me, from various quarters, in the thirteen years that have since followed to the present day.

The "Victory of Divine Goodness", published ten years ago, continued the same line of thought, in connexion with the special perplexities of a private correspondent, personally unknown to me, and with the two main subjects of Atonement and Judgment to Come. But nearly one half of the work, the notes on Coleridge's Confessions, had no proper unity with the rest, and the letters to my correspondent were too fragmentary in form to deal worthily with so many subjects of high importance. The remarks on eternal judgment gave birth to strange misrepresentations, of which I do not seek to revive the memory. But I have here included the two Essays on the Atonement and Eternal Judgment, somewhat revised, in the series of subjects treated in the former edition of the Difficulties, so that the treatise will now range onward from the Creation and the Fall to the Redemption and the New Creation still to come. I have also prefixed a brief summary of the direct Scripture evidence for the doctrine, and some examples of the strong and deep prejudices awakened by it in leading writers of the present day. These will prove, I think, convincingly, the great need for such an effort as I have honestly made, in entire dependence on the teaching of the Word and the Spirit of God, to clear away false representations, and causeless additions to the truth Divinely revealed, to show its harmony with other great truths no less plainly, and even more fully taught, and thus to strengthen the defences of the Christian faith; and show that, even when clouds and darkness are round about the Almighty Creator, justice and judgment are the habitation of his throne, that his goodness is infinite, and his name is Love. While I humbly desire his forgiveness for every defect in my treatment of themes so high and mysterious, I commend the work, in its enlarged and revised form, to his favour and blessing, in the prayer once offered before :—"May the great Head of the Church, all whose works are truth, and his ways judgment, accept the humble offering, and make it minister to the glory of his excellent name, and the ripening and perfecting of the faith of his true servants."

TRINITY PARSONAGE, CAMBRIDGE,
September, 1876.

INTRODUCTION.

ON THE KNOWLEDGE OF GOD.

THE existence of One First Cause, powerful, wise, good, and holy, the Lord and Governor of the universe, is the foundation of all natural and revealed religion. It is the fountain out of which every other truth must really flow. "I AM THAT I AM. I AM THE FIRST AND THE LAST, and beside me there is no God." In these messages, God has announced to mankind his own prerogative of unchangeable, eternal, essential being. All creatures, compared with Him, are less than nothing, and vanity. His majesty dwarfs the splendour of all created beauty; and the universe, apart from Him who formed and sustains it, would almost appear, to the eye of reason, like a shadowy dream.

But there may be a great contrast between the certainty and dignity of a truth in itself, and the clearness with which it is apprehended by men. What is first and highest in its own nature, may possibly be latest in the order of human knowledge. The laws on which the movements of our earth, and the changes of its seasons depend, existed for long ages before their discovery. So also that primal truth, on which all others are secretly

B.   A suspended, may require slow and successive steps of thought, before we can reach the mountain-top where we can gaze on it with a clear and steadfast vision. The child becomes familiar with many objects, its toys and playthings, and the countenances of its nurse and parents, before it knows the source of the light by which all these are made visible, or has ever beheld the calm beauty of the rising or setting sun. And when it is seen at last, its brightness must be tempered by clouds, or by the mists of the morning or evening sky; and the number is small of those who borrow the help of art, in order to gaze directly on its meridian brightness. In like manner, to behold with steadfast and unclouded gaze the true and uncreated Light is a hard and high attainment. Its brightness dazzles and confounds the reason of man. It must be seen reflected upon the objects of earth, or tempered with some veil which heavenly love itself has provided, before the vision of sinful creatures can endure its glory.

This contrast between the nature of the truth, and our faint and variable apprehensions of it, has led to some perplexity with regard to the evidence on which it rests. The pious mind shrinks from the thought that a doctrine so momentous should be viewed merely as a high probability. It claims for it instinctively some absolute demonstration.

Now demonstrative reasoning usually descends from generals to particulars, from causes to their effects, from principles to their necessary consequences. But when we reverse the process, and ascend from effects to causes, the result often appears to be tentative and imperfect. After much labour and a wide induction, we arrive at conclusions not absolutely, but only partially true; which have to be modified by further investigation, and a more comprehensive range of experience. Must, then, our faith in the Being of God be of this vague, uncertain kind? Is it only, after all, a probable and imperfect guess, instead of a sure and firm foundation for our whole moral being?

To remove this doubt, we must distinguish between partial and absolute knowledge. To infer a cause from an effect, and an effect from a cause, are processes in themselves equally sure and demonstrative. Whether we ascend or descend in the chain of reasoning, it is the nature of the links alone which determines the degrees of evidence. But while we may deduce a large variety of effects from a single cause, clearly defined and fully known, our knowledge of the cause must be imperfect and limited, if it be gained from a few effects only. A planet acted upon by a constant central force, varying inversely as the square of the distance, will describe an ellipse, with the areas, measured from the focus, proportional to the time. The cause being assumed to act undisturbed, the result is capable of a strict and absolute demonstration. And conversely, if such motions are observed through one revolution of the planet, the existence of a central force, varying by such a law and no other, may be concluded with equal certainty. But we cannot infer that this force will remain constant through successive revolutions. It may vary by a periodical and intermittent action. We cannot be sure that the same force, or any force, will be exercised on a body in a different plane of motion, or that the same law of intensity will extend to all distances, nearer or more remote, in the same plane. These extensions of the law are inferences from other facts, or from the observed simplicity of natural laws in general, and may be either confirmed or disproved by the lessons of a wider and more prolonged experience. In most departments of physical science, these hypothetical extensions of laws derived from a partial experience will sometimes prove erroneous, and thereby will seem to reflect doubt upon the very process of inductive reasoning. But this is a mere illusion. The reasoning is firm and demonstrative on its own nature, and only fails us, when we mingle our imperfect guesses with the actual results of pure and simple induction.

Now these remarks apply to the higher truths of the moral universe. No finite being can fully comprehend the nature of God. It is a mystery too deep for us to fathom in all its real profundity. He "dwelleth in light which no man can approach unto, whom no man hath seen or can see, the King of kings and Lord of lords." All our conceptions must be very imperfect, and fall far short of the glorious reality. We cannot, by searching, find out the Almighty unto perfection. It is only a faint whisper of his greatness that our ears can receive; but "the thunder of his power who can understand?" But those separate elements, which, when combined, form our highest conceptions of his being, may be separately capable of pure and absolute demonstration, as well as those intermediate steps by which we rise to them; although few, comparatively, may apprehend the whole of them, or combine them harmoniously into one pure and perfect idea of Supreme and Absolute Goodness. Hence may arise all the existing varieties of religious faith, in which truths, demonstrable and sure in themselves, are either seen through a mist, or held down in unrighteousness; so that "gods many, and lords many," usurp the homage due to Jehovah; or dark shadows, where his supreme power is owned, obscure his perfections and his glory. Wherever superhuman and unseen powers are worshipped, which, in the view of the worshippers themselves, have not supreme dominion or essential being, the religious instinct is in exercise, but stops short entirely of its proper object; and the first great commandment is transgressed, "Thou shalt have none other gods but me." Where the worship is directed to a Being supreme above all others, but under false representations, whether of the senses or the imagination, by which his true character is obscured or denied, there is a breach of the second commandment, and a more or less aggravated form of religious idolatry. But if the separate truths, which underlie this mass of religious instincts and traditions, are cleared from the dross of human errors, each of them will be found capable of a true demonstration by principles which lie at the foundation of our daily life; while their various rays, all converging to one centre, will reveal to our minds that Awful and Glorious Presence, which decks itself with light as a garment, and sits enthroned on the riches of the universe.

And first, that every event and every object must have some cause, is a principle so rooted in our minds, that our whole life involves its hourly application. We are conscious of it in the motions of our own bodies. We discern it in all the changes of physical nature, and apply it by an unalterable instinct to the actions and conduct of our fellow-men. Hence we ourselves, and the objects that surround us, must have some cause of our being. But we are conscious that we ourselves are not the cause. We did not make ourselves, nor create the objects which we see around us. Experience shows, as plainly, that our fellow-men, living with us, are not the cause of their own being, nor of the outward world which is our common home. If we refer to our parents, and prolong the chain

backward, we have no key at all to the existence of the
lower creatures, and have advanced no nearer to a full
and adequate explanation. The whole series of generations, and the generative power itself, are effects that
need to be explained. If we conceive some being, finite
and mutable, a mere Demiurge of limited faculties, and
born in time, yet endued with might and wisdom to
fashion the lower creatures, and give birth to the whole
human race, a higher Cause will still be required to
account for his existence. Reason, when once it wakes to
the simple truth, that every effect requires a cause, leads
us upward, with swift and irresistible progress, to the feet
of the Almighty. It cannot rest till it has pointed us to
one great First Cause, on which all lower causes and all
created beings must depend. There may be, for aught we
can tell by experience, "gods many and lords many," unseen by the eye of man, and superior to human power;
but there is and must be one Only God, of whom are all
things, the Fountain of Being, and self-existent cause of
all created things.

Again, we are conscious to ourselves, and observe the
presence in others, of a faculty of design. We can choose
for ourselves objects of desire, and combine various means
for their attainment. Life is one stream of human purposes, hopes, and fears, either disappointed or fulfilled. In
the choice of ends to be pursued, and of the means for
securing them, we perceive by experience the widest
varieties, both in ourselves and our fellow-men. To some
plans we give the title of wisdom, to others, of folly. But
whether successful or unsuccessful, whether wise or foolish, the idea of design is the same. We are conscious of
it in ourselves. We perceive it, without a shade of doubt,
in the conduct of our fellow-men, and even in the instincts

of the lower creatures. But we also discover the clearest
traces of it in the events of Providence, and in the frame
of the world, where we can trace it to no human agency
whatever. Reason tells us plainly, that these marks of
design prove the existence of a Designer. Still further,
the same reason teaches us that the first cause of existences, themselves capable of design, and gifted with
various degrees of wisdom, must itself be wise. A blind,
unconscious fate could never be an adequate cause of conscious wisdom. And thus, by a double inference, which
grows in clearness the longer our thoughts dwell upon it,
we are assured that the First Cause must be also the
Supreme Architect and Designer of the universe, and that
the Creator of beings gifted with the faculty of wisdom
and foresight must Himself be the True and Absolute
Wisdom.

But, further, we are moral agents. We are conscious
of a will and power of choice, and cannot avoid passing
judgment on ourselves and others with regard to the
manner in which this power of choice is exercised. We
praise and blame, we approve and condemn. We do this
by an instinct which it is impossible to control, and the
sophists who strive to quench it are themselves unwilling
witnesses to its mighty and unquenchable power. The
Epicurean kindles into zeal when he denounces in superstition the guilty curse of mankind; and the Materialists,
who would resolve our being into a concourse of atoms,
often inveigh against the crimes of priests and kings with
a strange and instructive inconsistency. The moral instinct, violently repressed in its natural outlets, forces
itself a passage some other way. The deep-seated contrast of moral good and evil lies at the root of all our
daily judgments. The conscience of all men, as the

Apostle tells us, bears witness to its truth, and their reasonings among themselves, while they accuse or else excuse one another. But the same law of thought, which compels us to look up through all the long vista of second causes, till we reach one First Cause, self-caused and absolute, constrains us no less to trace all derived and partial goodness in the creatures to a perfect and absolute goodness, the uncreated and hidden Fountain, whence every stream of blessing must flow. And thus Power, Wisdom, Goodness, in one common source, in which every one is found absolute and perfect—the First Cause, the Supreme Architect, the Purely Good—together constitute our fundamental conception of the Godhead. These three letters compose his ineffable and glorious Name, who is the Maker of all things, the only wise God, a Being of spotless holiness and perfect love.

There is nothing arbitrary, uncertain, or hypothetical in this threefold cord of reason, which binds the soul of man to the footstool of the Almighty. We may, through a careless and ungodly heart, stop short in the ascent of wisdom, and thus fail to attain, even in its bare outline, this knowledge of the true and only God. We may rise, for instance, to the apprehension of many second causes, higher than man, and unseen by our bodily eyes, and rest on these, as the agents in all the events of Providence and the changes of the outward world. These secondary powers may be many in number, as well as limited and imperfect in their power. Born in time, like ourselves, they may be conceived subject to changes and decay. We may take the signs of wisdom and design in the universe, and distribute them among these unseen powers. We may also ascribe to them distinct forms of moral excellence, or chequer these with varieties of moral defect, such as we meet with among our fellow-men. In such a creed we have the system of Polytheism. So far as it recognises the existence of such higher powers, it may be a truth. But it is not *the* truth to which reason conducts the patient inquirer. It stops short at the foot of the mount. And hence, in an age of active thought, such a system of Polytheism must either sink into mere Atheism, or rise into a pure Theism, as the sensual or spiritual element prevails in the minds of men. Jove, the son of Saturn, who reigned, by deposing his own father, on the snowy heights of Ida and Olympus, amidst a family of gods and goddesses, must either give place to the atoms of Democritus and the philosophy of Epicurus, or be transmuted into a higher object of faith—the Living One and the Supreme, whose offspring we all are,

"Undo nil majus generatur ipso,
    Nec viget quidquam simile aut secundum."

The object of a heathenish worship is here displaced by a dim apprehension of the true and only God, ignorantly worshipped, though still practically unknown. Reason lies down and sleeps midway on her journey, and Polytheism is the child of her dreams. She awakes and pursues her journey, and the morning light of heaven dawns upon her footsteps, and greets her with a vision of the blessed and only Potentate, the true Lord of heaven and earth.

Again, we may trace up all effects to a great First Cause, and forbear to dwell on those proofs of design of which we are conscious to ourselves, and of which the universe is full. Our conception will thus remain essentially and radically imperfect. Faith in such a Deity is vain and useless for every moral purpose. We are not believers in an All-wise God, but in a Supreme Fate—unwise, unconscious, and unreasoning—which acts with

relentless vigour, by some blind and unaccountable necessity. In this case there can be no providence, and no
moral government. There will brood over creation the
dark shadow of an Absolute Power, which works it knows
not why, and cares not how, and crushes in swift succession under its wheels the creatures to which it has given
birth. This creed of fatalism, though disguised, is often
the chief element in false religions. Compared with the
fatal Sisters, even Jove himself was feeble in the Greek
mythology. This serpent hid itself amidst the festoons of
flowers with which the Pagans wreathed the statues of
their divinities, and asserted a true and awful supremacy
over the practical faith of mankind.

But a further step may be taken, and the soul may
still come short of the fundamental truth of natural and
revealed religion. The outward and the inner world may
alike be recognised as full of the evidences of design. All
the rays of power and natural wisdom in the various
creatures may be seen converging upward to one common
source in whom they centre, and from whom they must
flow. The great First Cause is then owned to be a wise
and conscious Being, the Supreme Architect, the Natural
Governor of the universe. But the consciousness of moral
good and evil may still slumber; and hence the highest
and most distinguishing element may be wanting entirely
in our conception of the Supreme Being. Providence is
now recognised, but in forms of natural goodness alone.
From the minutest speck which the microscope discovers,
to the wide range of infinite space which the telescope
vainly seeks to explore, this Power revels in the display of
its ever-varied wisdom, amidst the mechanism of suns and
systems, and all the countless wonders of animal and
vegetable life. But no moral purpose is discerned in this

display of superhuman power and sagacity. We have only a Mechanician of unrivalled skill, who has formed the universe, like an immense toy-shop, to display with a capricious prodigality the inexhaustible resources of his mechanical ingenuity.

Such is the abstract Deity which meets us too often in the writings of natural philosophers, whenever they suffer their conscience to go to sleep amidst their profound scientific inquiries. Such students of nature fail to learn the first and simplest lesson of true religion, that God is no abstract and lifeless Being, but the Moral Governor of accountable creatures; perfect not only in natural wisdom, but in righteousness and holiness; supremely good, no less than supremely wise.

But when we reach the last mountain-top, from which the glory of the true and living God begins to dawn upon our spirits, new mists gather around us, and threaten to rob us of the vision, and plunge us into darkness again. The same deep instinct which reveals to us the contrast of moral good and evil, and compels our reason to ascribe perfect goodness to the Supreme Source of all being, discloses also the mournful fact, that moral evil does exist and prevail widely through the universe. How, then, can we explain this fact, if there be a God of infinite power and goodness? Surely, either the power or the will to remove it must be wanting. If the power, then how can God be Almighty? If the will, then how can He be infinitely good? The minds of men, as reasonable beings, would acquiesce readily in the simple and glorious truth, that there is a God, All-wise, Almighty, and All-perfect; but this fact, the existence and power of moral evil, and that for long ages, flings them back into sceptical doubt and perplexity. The infidel appeals to it with a kind of

malicious joy, to warrant his own unbelief; and even the
devout Christian is often afraid to trust himself into these
deep waters, and, while conscious of a doubt still unsatis-
fied, is tempted to stifle it, if possible, by a violent effort of
the will.   But, in spite of these efforts, the doubt and
perplexity still recur.   This dark shadow, which shut the
heathen world in a hopeless gloom, hovers still over the
various schools of Christian theology; and the bright discovery of Divine love in the Gospel has not succeeded in
driving away entirely this pall of night from the spiritual
heavens.

When the faith of the Christian borrows the aid of
reason to remove the darkness, it tends to lose itself in
two opposite labyrinths, from which no outlet is found.
In one direction we encounter the Manichean doctrine,
that there are two original independent powers of good
and evil, the Ormusd and Ahriman of Zend theology,
which contend with balanced might for the dominion of
the universe.   In the other, we meet a Christian fatalism,
which only avoids the admission of an evil Power, by
introducing dualism into the bosom of the Godhead.   The
Supreme Sovereign is placed above the laws of righteousness, which He has implanted in the heart of his own
creatures.   Moral good and evil, happiness and misery,
salvation and ruin, are viewed as alike the results of his
arbitrary and sovereign will.   Between the Scylla of Manichean heresy, and the deeper gulf of this blasphemous
perversion of truth, which makes God himself the author
of all evil, how shall we guide the vessel of our reason in
safety, so as not to make shipwreck of our faith?   How
shall we avoid either limiting the almighty power, or
denying the spotless and perfect holiness, of the God whom
our hearts inwardly adore?

All the difficulties which obscure the wisdom and goodness of their Maker from the eyes of men, and tempt numbers to doubt even the firm and simple conclusion of awakened reason, when it assures them of his power and Godhead, resolve themselves into this one question —the nature of moral evil, and the righteousness and goodness of God in the moral government of the world. It is the presence of moral evil alone, which disposes men to doubt the goodness and wisdom of the Most High. It is the fact of moral evil, borne with, but not removed, which gives force to all their questionings against the ways of Providence. It is the solemn threatening of judgment to come upon the workers of iniquity, which forms the stumbling-block of the unbeliever in coming to the word of God, and persuades him that the Bible contradicts the pure instincts of perfect benevolence. If this one problem were solved, all other petty cavils would die away of themselves. While darkness broods over it, these spectres will start up in ten thousand forms; and every part of God's word, every act of his providence, will be a fresh occasion for unwilling perplexity in the humble, and for open blasphemy in the proud and arrogant sinner. It is a problem, too, with which it seems impossible to deal separately, by natural reason and the light of supernatural revelation. Without the light which the word of God supplies, we cannot even make any approach to a solution of the immense difficulty. And when we take Revelation for our guide, the darkness which seems removed in some directions, thickens and deepens in others; and all the miseries and wrongs of the present life seem often more tolerable to the awakened reason, than the prospect of the retribution which is declared to await the rebellious in the world to come.

It is comparatively an easy task to rove through all creation, and come back laden with evidence of the Divine power and greatness, and of the bounty displayed in the formation of innumerable worlds. The mind, enriched with the treasures of science, and gifted with eloquence, may compose a beautiful and glowing panegyric on the countless tokens of the Divine beneficence. But amidst all the beauty of these lovely songs, the plague-spot of the spirit will remain untouched and unhealed, unless a cure can be found for those cruel suspicions which flow out of the prevalence of sin and sorrow in the present life, and the repeated warnings of strange judgment to come hereafter on the workers of iniquity. If further light, however feeble and imperfect, can be thrown upon this mystery, it will be a real and lasting boon to the Church of Christ, and, indirectly, a new power for the triumphs of Divine truth in the world. If this mystery remains in total darkness, all declamation on the benevolence of the Almighty, and attempts to answer cavils, are almost utterly vain. The believer must be content to own himself a child, who cannot answer the aspersions thrown out against the Father whom he loves, but believes that his Father will himself scatter them in due time.

To throw some light upon this great problem, and thereby to vindicate the wisdom and goodness of Jehovah, is the aim of the following Essay. May He, who searches the deep things of God, bestow a blessing upon the effort, and enable us to pierce a little further, in the spirit of reverence, into the thick darkness which surrounds the throne of the Most High!

CHAPTER I.

ON THE POWER OF GOD.

THE word of God reveals to us the existence of holy
angels, who delight in the service of their Creator, and
render Him the tribute of their continual praise. It
speaks of a time when man himself was upright and sinless, and surrounded by the beauty of an earthly Paradise.
And when it withdraws the veil from the future, we see
multitudes of our race recovered to perfect holiness, and
dwelling in the presence of God, where they enjoy a happiness undimmed by one cloud of sorrow.

Now we may conceive a plan of Providence where
nothing should meet the eye but these joyful images of
peace and purity. We may picture to ourselves the
worlds, which science reveals in the depths of infinite
space, all peopled in succession with holy beings, like unfallen man or sinless angels, who should abide in spotless
innocence and perfect love for ever. From these innumerable worlds we may imagine the hosannahs of holy
worship to rise perpetually before the throne of the Most
High; while the variety of wisdom which we perceive
among the lower creatures might only be a type of ever-
varying forms of love and sympathy, which should be
displayed in the intercourse of these reasonable creatures

with each other, in the feast of reason and the flow of
deep affections through the course of eternal ages. In
this wide range of blessedness, we may assume that not
one trace shall be found of rebellion against the Almighty
Creator, and that not one wail of sorrow and misery ever
mingles with the chorus of universal thanksgiving. It is
natural to inquire, Would not such a universe have been
far preferable to what we see around us, or to that che-
quered prospect, of mercy mingled with awful judgments,
which Christianity discloses in its visions of the world to
come ?   Does it not meet all the instincts of a true benevolence ?   Is it not a scheme worthy of Infinite Goodness
to devise, and for Infinite Power to execute ?   Where is
the power of God, if He were unable to frame a universe
full of unmingled happiness ?   Where his perfect goodness,
if He were able to frame a world, in which the happiness
of every creature, though lower in degree, would have
been pure and unmingled like his own; and preferred to
let in upon them a flood of evils, that would involve immense multitudes in present sorrow and eternal ruin ?

This difficulty, which has haunted thoughtful and loving hearts for ages, has been stated, with almost malicious
clearness, by the sceptic historian, in his account of the
creed of Zoroaster.   "The appearance of moral and physical evil had established the two principles in the ancient
philosophy and religion of the East.   A thousand shades
may be devised in the nature and character of Ahriman,
from a rival God to a subordinate demon, from passion
and frailty to pure and perfect malevolence.   But, in spite
of our efforts, the goodness and the power of Ormusd are
placed at opposite extremities of the line, and every step
that approaches the one must recede in equal proportion
from the other."

The solution of this difficulty, which seems to be most usual among Christian divines, is by no means satisfactory to the thoughtful mind. It has been often assumed for a self-evident truth, that God, by virtue of his omnipotence, could easily have hindered the first entrance of evil into his moral creation ; and that He could also banish it in a moment by a simple act of his sovereign will, now that its dark shadows have overspread the universe. But it is alleged that there are wise reasons why evil has been permitted, and is still allowed to continue. A greater good is hereby to be secured in the end, and the various attributes of the Creator are to be more signally displayed in the severity of his justice, and the riches of his grace.

There are two reasons which conspire to prove the insufficiency of this explanation, however current it may be among a large class of Christian divines. And first, if the omnipotence of God makes it certain that the entrance of evil might have been prevented, or that, after its first entrance, it might still be crushed in a moment, will it not equally prove that the end proposed might also have been gained by a simple act of the Divine will, without recourse to a process so painful and terrible ? If God is almighty to destroy at once every trace of moral evil, is He not also almighty to bestow at once every varied form of moral excellence, instead of leaving them to be slowly and arduously gained, through years of perilous probation, and long, dark ages of abounding iniquity and sorrow ? There can be no room for a wise choice of means to attain some worthy end, if the end be just as attainable without any means whatever. In this case wisdom is only a mockery and a name. The whole apparatus of means becomes a laborious and troublesome superfluity. Warnings, promises, invitations, threatenings, examples, precepts, are alike unreal and collusive, if the true meaning of Omnipotence is a power to supersede them all at any moment, and to secure the very end proposed by these various agencies and influences, by a pure and simple volition of the Almighty.

But there is another, and perhaps even a still weightier, objection to this view. Besides abolishing the very possibility of wisdom, it seems directly to impeach the Divine goodness. An Apostle has taught us, concerning those who do evil that good may come—"their condemnation is just." The general conscience of mankind has affixed the stamp of blasphemy on the doctrine that God is the Author of evil. Now the word of God, the true standard of moral judgment to his creatures, places sins of omission and commission very much on the same level. " To him that knoweth to do good, and doeth it not, to him it is sin." "If thou forbear to deliver them that are drawn unto death, and them that are appointed to be slain, doth not he that pondereth the heart consider it ?—and he that keepeth thy soul, doth he not know it ?—and will he not render to every man according to his works ?"

The law of duty, which God enjoins upon his creatures in this solemn appeal, must be the transcript of his own moral perfections. To forbear to do the good, which is within our power, is here placed on the same footing of crime with the active working of evil. But the alleged purpose, that good may come, will not shield active wrong-doing from deserved condemnation. How, then, can it be a moral justification for the forbearance of good, which is really in our power to be done ? If the Almighty has forborne to deliver myriads upon myriads of his reasonable creatures, who are ready to be slain with a worse than temporal death, when a simple act of will would alone suffice for their deliverance, how can we avoid the conclusion

that He has done, on the largest scale, what He proclaims
to be an inexcusable crime, and threatens to visit with his
severest displeasure? Do we not, by such an hypothesis,
make God too much like ourselves, whose conscience often
slumbers under the mere neglect of duty, while it would
revolt from the direct commission of open crimes?

When this conviction has taken root in the mind, that
the entrance of moral evil, and its long continuance, are
due to the active agency or passive connivance of the
Almighty, all the stupendous works of his love, to repair
the miseries of the fall, quickly lose their power over the
heart. The Gospel of Christ can then hardly escape from
the charge of being a vanity and an illusion. For can we
reasonably ascribe the perfection of wisdom and goodness
to conduct, which we should impute at once, in our fellow-
creatures, to a criminal folly? Suppose that a parent has
it in his power to secure the happiness, obedience, and
virtue of all his children, from their first infancy, and that
he prefers to leave them all to spend years in brutish vice
or wicked passions, and many of them to perish in their
vices at the last, that some may be recovered through a
fearful course of suffering; in order, by this means, to show
his wisdom and sagacity in the remedial measures he
afterwards employs, and which have only a limited and
partial success; could we praise him for his wisdom and
goodness? Should we not rather condemn him for de-
fective benevolence even to his own children, and be
ready to account his very acts of kindness, to reclaim
these prodigals, a course of laborious folly? Yet is not
this the very charge which would lie, in spite of our
efforts, against the perfections of the Godhead, if we
accept the views which have been widely current with
regard to the true meaning of Omnipotence?

"God could, doubtless, convert and save all men and all devils; but He has wise reasons for not doing it." These words of a judicious commentator express the popular impressions of our modern theology relative to the power of God. The Scriptures, it is evident, have nowhere directly affirmed what is here said to be an undoubted truth. It is an inference of human reason from a Divine attribute. Now such inferences require great caution, that we may not confound mischievous illusions, due to our own ignorance, with the real truth of God. The world has plainly been full of misconceptions of the Divine wisdom and goodness. Is it likely that its current and popular notions of Divine power would alone be free from the infection of serious error? One falsehood, received blindly for an undoubted truth, may possibly infect the whole system of theology, and cast a dark and gloomy shadow around the throne of the Most High. And since the alternative, here examined, wears this threatening aspect towards two main perfections of the Godhead, ought we not, before receiving it into our creed, to search very narrowly into the secret assumption on which it rests?

What, then, is the true meaning of the Divine Omnipotence? Is it the power to do whatever is conceivable by the thoughts of men, or simply whatever is possible in its own nature? Or do both definitions agree, so that every hypothesis, capable of being propounded by the human faculties, is proved to be possible by that circumstance alone?

If the mind of man were perfect in knowledge, no conception it forms could ever involve contradictory elements. But this is not really the case. An ignorant and erring fancy may associate many things in words which are quite incompatible. The greater our ignorance, the wider must be the sphere of these illusions. It is true that, in these cases, the mind cannot form a clear and full conception. This is the reason why the real incongruity remains concealed. But it is plain that such impossibilities may be accounted possible, and may pass current for a while in the forum of human speculations. The child who has just learned the meaning of an angle or triangle, may think it possible and easy to construct a three-sided figure, whose angles shall be greater or less than two right angles; or to vary the dimensions of a right-angled triangle, so that the square on its hypothenuse shall exceed those on its sides by a definite quantity. So, too, the novice in dynamics may conceive such motions to be impressed on a system of atoms by their mutual action alone, that their centre of gravity may revolve in a circle. The geometer knows that these problems are impossible in their own nature. They do not come within the province of Omnipotence to execute, but of Omniscience to discern their inherent contradiction. Thousands of similar examples may be drawn from the range of pure science, and prove that many things are really contradictory and impossible, in which the eye of ignorance can see no contradiction whatever.

This distinction, which science reveals to us in the material universe, between things possible and impossible in their own nature, or in other words, between essential truth and essential falsehood, is clearly extended in the Scriptures to the very nature of the Godhead. "God, that cannot lie," is one of the glorious titles of Jehovah, which the Apostle of the Gentiles sets before us to confirm our faith. We are reminded that "if we believe not, he abideth faithful, he cannot deny himself." And to

the character of essential truth, another Apostle adds the
like attribute of essential goodness: "Let no man say,
when he is tempted, I am tempted of God; for God cannot be tempted of evil, neither tempteth he any man."
There are things conceivable by the mind of man, which
are not possible to the Almighty, because they would involve a denial and contradiction of the real perfection of
his own being. The Judge of all the earth cannot do
wrong. · He, who is a God of truth, and without iniquity,
cannot behold iniquity with pleasure. "He is not a man,
that he should repent." He cannot reverse his own essential perfections. His name is I AM, and He cannot
by an act of will, cease to be. His name is Love, and He
cannot become hatred. His name is God the only wise,
and He cannot be deceived. That glorious title, by which
the seraphim adore Him continually, implies his essential
holiness, which makes it impossible that He should be
subjected to error, or tempted with evil. He is the true
Light, and all darkness and shadow must lie perpetually
without his all-perfect Being; and to suppose Him capable, by an act of his own will, of introducing them into
that Holy of holies, is nothing else than a contradiction
and lying blasphemy.

But this principle, being once established in the lowest
walk of creation, amidst its material elements, and also
with reference to the Creator himself, must be further
applicable to all his moral creatures, and the relations
they bear to one another, and to the First Cause on
whom they depend. Good and evil, wisdom and folly,
in all moral agents, are no changeable, arbitrary things.
If their seat is the bosom of God, their voice, resounding
through all creation, is the harmony of the universe.
A woe is denounced on all those who put darkness for

light, and light for darkness; who put bitter for sweet,
and sweet for bitter; while it is the very test of spiritual
progress to "have the senses exercised to discern good
and evil." If these foundations be destroyed, what can
the righteous do? But they never can be destroyed:
heaven and earth may pass away, but the deep foundations of God's holy law can never pass away. The essential contrast of moral goodness with all things evil
has its source in the perfection of the Divine nature,
but extends through the whole range of the intelligent
universe, and repeats itself, in ten thousand forms, through
all the various messages of the word of God.

What, then, is the true conception of Omnipotence,
so far as our dim-sighted faculties can apprehend so lofty
a truth? It may be summed up in the three main aspects of Creation, Providence, and Grace. It is a power,
first of all, to call innumerable creatures out of nothing,
by the simple fiat of the Divine Will, and to endow them
with various activities, by which they are differenced
from each other and from the Creator who bestows them,
and are gifted with a real though dependent being. The
power of God in creation ranges from the simplest monad
endued with a law of force, and so constituted a point
in the world of matter, to the seraph who veils his wings
in holy worship before the throne, and rejoices in the
union of a pure and large intelligence with the highest
fervour of love and the most intense activity of will. It
includes the mysterious gift of life, which can overflow
the narrow fountain wherein it is first contained, and
diffuse and multiply itself in the production of new
existences, resembling its own parent being. "He spake,
and it was done; he commanded, and it stood fast," is
the sublime formula of Creative Omnipotence, and our

imagination faints in the effort to conceive the vastness of its inexhaustible treasures.

But the Almighty Power of God is seen, further, in the work of Providence. And here it consists in the power to sustain and govern all creatures with absolute authority and control, according to their distinct natures, which God himself has bestowed. In the material world, it is the power to move, transport, and modify everything which He has created, from the mote which plays in the sunbeam, to the systems of innumerable worlds which science discovers, as they lie scattered, with a wild profusion of Divine bounty, through the depths of space. In the moral and spiritual world, it is the power to act on mind, in all its varieties, according to the essential laws of its constitution. It includes all varieties of moral suasion by motives addressed to the understanding and conscious will, with no other limit than may arise from the incapacity of the creature to apprehend the truth proposed, or the reluctance of the will to feel the power of the motives addressed to the heart. How far this limit may extend, is a subject for more profound inquiry. At present, it is enough to observe, that, even assigning these limits their fullest significance, they must leave a wide field for the harmonious exhibition of the Divine Wisdom and Omnipotence, in disposing all the events of life towards a consummation worthy of the God of love.

But Omnipotence may be conceived to have a distinct and higher sphere than the common arrangements of Providence, in the secret operations of Divine grace. It is clear that many creatures are really sunk in a fearful depth of moral evil. It is also evident that every gift of active powers must involve certain passive capabilities, which may be equally definite with the powers on which they depend. Every convex has its concave, and the curvature of the one determines that of the other, since they are two inseparable aspects of one and the same thing. Reason and experience combine to prove that the same powers which constitute man a moral agent, are joined in him with a capacity for being recovered to holiness again. It is reasonable to believe that this capacity may have its essential laws and limits, like those active powers of choice and will upon whose presence it seems to depend. And hence the Omnipotence of Divine grace denotes the sovereign power of God to recover fallen creatures out of their moral ruin, with no other limit than their essential capabilities of receiving the influences of his grace—a limit which we can only hope to determine by a reference, conjointly, to reason, experience, and the word of God.

The illusion which professes to enlarge the range of Divine Omnipotence—while it really contradicts its essential character, and, replacing the reality by a shadow, tends to impeach alike the wisdom and goodness of the Almighty—may thus present itself in three different forms. It may refer to the Being of God, to the work of Creation, or to his acts of Providence and Redemption. In its first variety, it must be met by the fundamental truth, that God cannot lie, that He cannot deny himself, that He cannot do iniquity, nor look on it with pleasure ; and that He cannot be tempted with evil, neither tempteth He any man. In its second form it must equally be resisted and exposed by the great truth —that God cannot create another God, equal to himself; that He cannot give his own glory to another, nor make any creature that shall not be essentially and eternally

subject to his own dominion, dependent on the great
First Cause, and obedient, either in act or obligation,
to the Supreme Lawgiver. In its third variety, as it
affects the relations of God to his own creatures, there
is a still wider range for a similar exercise of spiritual
wisdom, to discern between essential truth, and the false-
hoods which seem to be possible, and are only a deceit
and a lie. The Almighty himself can act upon his
creatures, only in conformity with the nature of the
being He has himself bestowed. Atoms or worlds may
be transported by his almighty fiat from place to place
with the speed of lightning; but they cannot be impressed
by arguments, allured by promises, or terrified by warnings. On the other hand, conscious spirits must be open
to every variety of moral suasion; and motives, high
as heaven and deep as hell, may be brought by the
Supreme Governor to bear upon the conscience and the
heart. But they cannot be the subject of merely mechanical impulses, like unconscious matter; and must be acted
upon, so far as we can comprehend, even by their Creator
himself, in strict agreement with the essential laws of
spiritual being. Repentance, the deepest work of grace,
is not a physical, but a moral change. Of such an effect
no physical force whatever is an adequate cause; and it
can result only from the moral suasion of warnings and
promises, hopes and fears, acting with conjoint and powerful energy upon the will, and subduing it into captivity
to the will of God.

From these principles some light may begin to dawn
upon the great problem which has ever exercised the
minds of men, and some help be gained to disperse the
clouds which have obscured alike the wisdom and goodness of God, by a crude and false conception of the Divine

Omnipotence. In the material world there are innumerable relations, which science discovers to be certain truths, and which Almighty Power can never transgress in its agency upon the natural universe, because Infinite Wisdom must have previously recognised their essential and unalterable validity. The same must be equally true in the field of moral government, though here our dim understandings may be less able to trace out the eternal truths, which the Most High God, in virtue of his perfect knowledge, must recognise as unalterably true in all his dealings with the souls He has made. In a subject so deep and mysterious, we are not at liberty to assume, from our crude notions of almightiness, that the prevention of the first entrance of moral evil must have been possible with God, or that it must be equally possible to banish it in a moment from the universe, by a bare, simple act of Divine volition. The lessons of experience, and the tenor of revelation, lie plainly and strongly the other way. There is a tone of earnestness and reality in all the appeals and reasonings of God with fallen creatures in his word, which sounds unavoidably like a painful and almost heartless mockery, if such an impression is received for a fundamental truth. Let us search, then, still further, with reverence and humility, into this obscure and perplexed labyrinth, and see whether we cannot discern some glimpses of light, by which to justify the ways and dealings of the Almighty with the children of men.

CHAPTER II.

ON THE NATURE OF EVIL.

" Every good gift, and every perfect gift, is from above, and cometh down from the Father of lights, with whom is no variableness, neither shadow of turning." His Being is the perfection of all goodness. So far as any creature derives its being from Him, it must be good—purely and simply good. But every created being has a further relation to that original nothingness, out of which it has been called by the fiat of God; and this relation gives birth to the idea of evil. It is the want or defect in the creature of some perfection which is found in the Creator. This defect, so far as it consists in the necessary limitation of created being, is metaphysical evil; while the changes which may result from the exercise of its imparted faculties are the source of natural and moral evil.

Let us begin with the lowest forms of existence, the atoms of the material world. Their goodness consists in their being itself, and the active power they have received from God. But the entire want of sense, thought, feeling, and intelligence, is the evil inseparable from their very constitution. A universe, composed of such atoms, and left to its own powers, could never rise above its own level. No trace of design, no tokens of

life, could reveal themselves in the unfathomable abyss
of confusion. Its only description would be that of our
poet, where the imaginary voyage of the Tempter is
portrayed—

> Before his eyes in sudden view appeared
> The secrets of the hoary deep, a dark
> Illimitable ocean, without bound,
> Without dimension, where length, breadth, and height,
> And time, and place are lost ; where eldest Night
> And Chaos, ancestors of Nature, hold
> Eternal anarchy, amidst the noise
> Of endless wars, and by confusion stand.

Such is the Chaos of the old cosmogonies. It brings
before us the idea of a whole universe of matter, without
form and void, where darkness broods upon the abyss, and
the Spirit has not begun to move upon the face of the
troubled elements with the energy of life and conscious
intelligence.

But now let us suppose that the laws and conditions of
this multitudinous mass have been selected, at first, by
the Great Architect, with a view to some higher purpose,
and to prepare the way for the production of nobler
forms of being. The time will come when, out of the
seemingly fortuitous mass of infinite confusion, order and
beauty will begin to appear. Suns and planets, and
systems of worlds, will gradually evolve themselves out
of the Chaos, where thought seemed to be lost in a gulf of
utter darkness. Matter and ether, condensing or diffused,
will issue in mysterious landscapes of light and beauty,
spread in rich profusion through the depths of infinite
space. And if it be one part of this great design, that
worlds shall be prepared in succession for the abodes of
life, there will be traceable, by an eye that can inspect
the whole universe, a gradual progress from undistinguish-

able and nebulous confusion, or volcanic and convulsive changes, to the quiet, tempered, and gentle harmony of planets like our own; where the seasons hold their mystic dance, and hills and valleys, capable of receiving various forms of life, are lit up with the splendour of suns, and moons, and stars, and drink water from the rain and dews of heaven.

But these traces of design in the material world refer chiefly to some higher forms of being, which these worlds and systems appear fitted to receive and sustain. This leads us a step higher in the ladder of creation. Vegetable life is a nobler gift than mechanical and chemical forces, such as the simple or compound atoms of matter exercise on each other. It seems to be a power of assimilation, striving after a prescribed standard of being, different in every species, capable of producing other derived powers like itself, and superior in its energy to the forces of those substances which it incorporates into its own being. Every seed, in its germination, seems to represent the essential duality of the universe. It strikes root downward into unconscious matter, from whence it derives the means of growth, and its own separate standing-place in creation. But it also strives upward into the air and light of heaven, where it develops the nobler part of its being. It seems, by a natural appetency, like the sunflower, to seek out those ethereal influences, by which alone it can be unfolded into maturity and perfection. This life of the plant is good and beautiful, as a gift of the bountiful Creator, and by its varied energy clothes the unconscious earth with its own beauty. But it is limited in its power to realize its own law, unconscious, and void of intelligence, and herein may be called evil. This defect is shown in abortive growths, where the powers of vegetation have been unable to surmount the opposing powers around them; as in the seeds which, in stony ground, have no depth of earth, and wither under the scorching sunbeam, or those which are choked in the thorny ground, and bring no fruit to perfection. We may see it also in the pathless and untrodden wilderness, where the luxuriant vegetation runs to waste through the absence of wise control; and putrid exhalations are bred from its decay, when its limited powers have exhausted and spent themselves, and resign its products back to the chaos of forces, which are always blindly at work in every part of the material world.

Let us turn from vegetables to animals, and we meet with a new and higher form of good and evil. The life of the lower animals, though hard to define, may perhaps be viewed as a power of perception, appetite, and self-motion, endowed with organs suitable for its exercise, and also with the power of reproduction. It is bounded, in all these faculties, by the range of the visible creation, is finite in its energies, incapable of apprehending spiritual and eternal truth, and is liable to decay when the limit of its natural activity has been attained. In these essential limitations of the animal life consists its metaphysical evil. And since these limitations are joined with a faculty of perception, and a certain power of choice, according to the variety of objects perceived, they involve the possibility of natural evil, or suffering, under a form which bears a close analogy with moral evil. For the animal instinct which pursues blindly its own satisfaction, when it involves the pain and death of another, resembles closely, in its working, the effect of wickedness in higher natures, that rejoice maliciously in the infliction of torture and misery. It differs from it, as metaphysical from moral evil, or the natural absence of a noble faculty, from its abuse and perversion. And since the higher animals are capable of instincts of attachment, and habits of obedience to a superior will, by which they seem to rise above their own level into the likeness of moral agents, so in these cases, the development of those instincts which cause injury to others awakens a dim notion of responsibility; and the words, vice, malice, and punishment, are instinctively applied to them in the current language of men. In proportion as any animal seems capable, under the eye of man, of apprehending a higher being than its own, we seem forced to recognize in it the dawn of a higher responsibility. The attachment of the faithful dog or horse to its master is the subject of instinctive praise; while the blind rage of the angry bull, or the bloodthirsty appetite of the tiger, that slaughters victims wantonly, when its hunger is appeased, excites instinctively a feeling of reprobation; and these emotions differ, perhaps, in degree, rather than in kind, from those which belong to moral agents. With the dawn of a moral faculty, which can own a master, and apprehend the supremacy of reason, we discern, as in a twilight, the entrance of new emotions of praise and blame, and a dim apparition of the great contrast between moral good and moral evil.

We now reach a higher point of observation. It has pleased the Almighty to create spiritual beings, endowed with conscience, reason, and will; capable of knowing, loving, and serving their Creator, of apprehending those eternal perfections which constitute his own felicity, and of gazing upon his infinite goodness and beauty. Such powers, in kind, appear to be the highest which it is possible for the Creator himself to bestow. But in extent and degree they may vary widely, from the weakness and nescience of

the new-born infant, to the powers of the loftiest archangel who stands before the throne of the Most High, and
who may hold a real vicegerency of dominion over ten
thousand thousand blessed and holy spirits in the kingdom of God.

Now the very existence of creatures endowed with
a power of free choice and a reasonable will, involves,
by necessary consequence, the idea of moral obligation.
Matter, in all its varieties, has a law imposed in the hour
of its creation, which it must obey. There is no choice,
and therefore no responsibility. But a moral agent, endowed with will, is not under such a physical necessity.
The idea of choice excludes it, and the word *must* applies
no longer. A sphere of active power is entrusted to its
own keeping, and it depends on its own choice what line
of conduct it shall pursue. Yet, since it is a creature, it
must be under law to its Creator. That law, having for
its object such a gift, by which the creature is found to
resemble the Creator, must also have for its rule that
essential perfection which is inseparable from the will of
God. Necessity being excluded by the nature of the gift,
obligation must supply its place. It is the only form of
law which is applicable to a creature so endowed; and since
a law there must be, or it would not be a creature, it
ought to be like God, because it is formed in his image;
it *ought* to do the will of God with a free and willing submission, because it is really the work of his hand. These
two maxims, derived from the very constitution of every
moral agent, created in the image of its Maker; that it
ought to serve Him with the complete submission of unconscious matter, which cannot choose but obey, and to
reflect his perfect goodness, with a liberty and purity like
those of the Creator himself; are the poles around which

B.   C

the whole universe of moral obligation must revolve perpetually.

Such agents, however noble the faculties with which
they are endowed, have limitations, which arise from the
fact that they are creatures, and constitute the metaphysical evil inseparable from their being.   They may be
immortal, but they are not from eternity.   They may be
pure, but they are not immutable.   They may have vast
powers of intelligence, but there is a bound to their actual
knowledge.   They may *apprehend* God, by a spiritual in-
tuition; but they cannot *comprehend* Him, or search out
all the depths of his infinite being.   They may be good,
wearing the image of their Maker; but, unlike Him, they
can be tempted with evil.   They may be dwelling in the
truth; but it is in their choice to abide in that truth, or to
depart from it into falsehood and darkness.   As created by
God, they have a Divine capacity for attaining higher and
higher degrees of moral insight and pure intelligence.   As
formed out of nothing, they may be called children of an
eternal night, and are equally capable of losing themselves
in an awful abyss of moral darkness.   The greatness of
the gifts bestowed upon them must measure the greatness
of their possible fall; since godlike powers abused, while
their natural excellence remains, must issue in a moral
chaos, abounding in every hateful form of diabolical wickedness.

Thus every creature of God, called out of nothing by
his almighty power, is like a planet in the sunlight, with
one hemisphere of natural good, and another of natural
evil.   As born of God, it is simply and purely good; as
born out of nothingness, it is purely and simply evil.   But
this evil, in the first state of creation, is not the same with
impurity or moral guilt.   In natural things, it is simply

defect, or the essential limitation of their being. In moral
agents, it is defectibility as well as limitation, and includes
the possibility of abusing the power of choice, that highest
gift of the bountiful Creator. Every creature, as soon as
created, casts from it a shadow on the side opposite to the
true Sun. From the very fact of its existence there
result inevitably many possibilities of evil. No simple
act, even of Almighty Power, can set aside this eternal
truth. But it is the very province of Infinite Wisdom to
dispose, overrule, and control all the creatures Omnipotence has made ; and, recognising the unalterable contrast
of light and darkness, of moral good and evil, so to unfold
it before the eyes of the moral universe, that the unfallen
may be maintained in their sinless purity ; and the fallen
and rebellious either recovered to purity again, or com-
pelled, while enduring the righteous judgment of the Most
High, to manifest, through eternal ages, the height and
depth of his victorious goodness.

CHAPTER III.

ON THE CREATION OF FREE AGENTS.

THE creation of moral and accountable beings is the first main step in those ways of Divine Providence, which have caused deep and perplexed questionings in thoughtful minds. If it was decreed, by the wisdom and goodness of the Most High, to create beings like angels and men, so nobly endowed, why did not his almighty power secure them against the fearful inroads of moral evil, with its present undeniable fruits of world-wide sorrow, and those still sadder results, which revelation sets before us, of everlasting shame and ruin? How can the permission of such a fall, if it could easily have been averted, be reconcilable with the simplest notion of benevolence? or what possible gain can result, that might not have been secured by the hand of Omnipotence, without an experience so unutterably awful? And again, if it be held that such a course was impossible in its own nature, the difficulty seems to recur in another form. Why did not the Almighty refrain from the exercise of his creative power, when He foreknew certainly that the issue, to an innumerable multitude, if not to the great majority of the spirits He made, would be to involve them in a dark abyss of hopeless despair and awful misery?

These difficulties were fully stated by the philosopher Bayle, at the close of the seventeenth century; and Leibnitz, in his "Theodicæa," has exercised the powers of his eminently fertile and profound intellect in furnishing a reply. If the views he there propounds were altogether just and valid, the only aim of a later writer should be to expand them into fuller detail, and bring them out into clearer relief by a popular exposition. But though no previous writer has perhaps done more to throw light upon the subject, his theory appears too metaphysical and cold, too closely mixed up with his baseless hypothesis of the pre-established harmony, and borders too nearly on the fatal maxim, that evil may be chosen on account of its supposed good results, to give full satisfaction to the intelligent Christian. The statement, however, he has made of the difficulties to be surmounted, will form a suitable preface to our further inquiries. May the Spirit, who searcheth even the deep things of God, go before us with a torch of heavenly truth, that we may not lose our footing amidst these ocean pathways of Divine Providence!

"It may be objected," the German philosopher observes, in prefacing his reply to the arguments of Bayle, "that all the reality, and what is called the substance of the act, in sin itself, is the work of God, since all creatures and all their acts derive from Him whatever is real in them; whence it might be inferred that He is not only the physical, but even the moral cause of sin; since He acts most freely, and does nothing without a perfect knowledge both of the thing and all its consequences. And it is not enough to say, that God has made himself a law to concur with the wills and resolutions of men; for, beside the strangeness of his having made such a law, of which He must have known the consequences, the chief difficulty, is, that it seems the evil will itself could not exist without some concurrence, and even predetermination on his part, which contributes to excite this will in man, or any other reasonable being. For an action, though evil, is not the less dependent upon God. Whence it might be inferred, finally, that God does all things without distinction, the good and the evil; unless we admit two principles, with the Manicheans.

"But even if God only concurred with a general concurrence, it is enough, it may be said, to render Him a moral cause of evil, that nothing happens without his permission. And, to say nothing of the fall of angels, He knows all that will happen, if He places man in such and such circumstances after He has created him, and still He does not forbear to place him in them. Man is exposed to temptations, to which it is known that he will yield, and thereby be the cause of frightful evils; that by this fall the whole human race will be infected, and put under a kind of necessity of sinning, which has been called Original Sin; that the world will hereby be brought into a strange confusion; that by this means sickness and death will be introduced, with a thousand other calamities, which affect both the good and the evil; that wickedness will reign, and virtue be oppressed here below; and that thus there will almost seem to be no Providence. But it is much worse, when we consider the life to come; since only a small number of men will be saved, and all the rest will perish eternally. Besides, these men, destined to salvation, will have been drawn from the corrupted mass by a choice without reason, whether we say that God had regard to their future good actions, their faith, or their works; or it is affirmed that He chose to give them these good qualities, because He had predestined them to salvation. For though it is said, in the more mitigated systems, that God has been willing to save all men; and is allowed, in those more generally received, that He made his Son to assume human nature, to expiate their sins, so that all who believe in Him with a lively and lasting faith will be saved; it still remains true that this lively faith is a gift of God; that we are dead to all good works, and that it needs preventing grace to excite our will. And whether election be the cause or consequence of the design of God, to give faith, it still remains true that He gives faith or salvation to whomsoever He pleases, without there appearing to be any reason for his choice, which only falls upon a very small number of men. So that it is a terrible judgment, that God, having given his Only-begotten Son for the whole human race, and being the only Author and Master of the salvation of men, notwithstanding saves so few, and leaves all the rest to the devil, his enemy, who torments them for ever, and makes them curse their Creator, although they were all created to show forth His goodness, justice, and other perfections. And this result is the more frightful, since all these men are miserable through eternity, only because God exposed their parents to a temptation which He knew they would not resist; and that this sin is inherent and imputed to men, before their will has part in it; that this hereditary vice determines their wills to commit actual sins, and a multitude of men, infants and adults, who have never heard of Jesus Christ, die before receiving the help that is needful to rescue them from this gulf of sin, and are condemned to be for ever rebels against God, and engulfed in horrible misery, with the most wicked of all creatures; although in reality these men have not been more wicked than others, and perhaps some of them less guilty than a part of the elect, who have been saved by a grace irrespective of character, and enjoy thereby an eternal felicity, which they never deserved."

Such are the serious difficulties which appear to lie against the scheme of Providence, as experience opens it before us; or as deducible, in the judgment of many theologians, from the statements of the Christian revelation. The first main subject to which they refer is the creation of free agents, with the foresight, or even the fore-appointment of their fall, and of all its fatal consequences of misery and ruin.

The solution of this first difficulty, which Leibnitz has proposed, is of the following nature. The wisdom and goodness of God require that out of all possible worlds or systems of Providence He should choose the best. But the essential truth of things implies that a world into which moral evil enters, and enters widely, is really best on the whole, since a greater good results from its permission. Therefore the wisdom of God requires that He should permit the entrance of evil, and forbids that exercise of Omnipotence by which alone it could have been averted. This permission is not the same with direct causation, since evil, from its very nature, can have no other than a deficient cause. It is also free from all moral blame, because its real motive is the purpose of securing a greater good, than would be otherwise possible to be achieved.

So far as this theory recognises the perfect wisdom of God's providence, it commends itself instinctively to the natural conscience. But the main difficulty remains untouched—how a world in which sin and sorrow have made such immense ravages can really be the best of all possible worlds. What is that greater good, for the sake

of which innumerable beings, capable of immortal happiness, are exposed to temptation, sunk in the depths of
sin, and consigned to a gulf of eternal misery? This
greater good must have respect, either to the glory of
God or the happiness of creation. But is it not more
glorious for the Divine goodness to delight in sustaining
the universe in unmingled and perfect bliss, than to have
the hosannahs of praise and joy mingled with the smoke
of perpetual torment, and the wail of ceaseless despair?
And is not the same alternative, while it would reflect
more brightly the glory of the Divine goodness, equally
conducive to the fullest happiness of all creation? The
antithesis, then, remains in its full force and perplexity.
You say that the present world is the best possible, because only such could proceed from a Being infinitely
good and wise. We affirm, the objector may retort, that
it is not the best possible, because, without perplexing
ourselves with subtle inquiries, or losing ourselves in the
infinite, we can conceive one plainly more conducive to
the Divine glory, and to the happiness of creation. That
world so clearly to be preferred is one over which moral
evil should never be suffered to cast its dark and hateful
shadows. It is one where the Almighty, by his sovereign
power, should at once unveil to countless numbers of sinless and happy spirits all those glorious perfections, which
now only a few of them attain to perceive and enjoy, after
a long and perilous course of probation, wherein multitudes of their fellow-creatures are sunk and stranded for
ever.

The only way in which this objection can be parried
is by an intermediate hypothesis of the following character.
We may conceive that it is competent to the Divine power
to sustain all moral agents in a state of purity and sinless

perfection, but not to endow them, in this case, with all
the wisdom and holiness, or the comprehension of the
Divine goodness, which results from the permitted entrance and continuance of sin. It may thus be urged that
the higher bliss of the redeemed, and the fuller display of
the Divine attributes, in their depths of holy justice and
heights of victorious grace, more than compensate for
those mournful and terrible results which flow from the
actual permission of moral evil.

This is, perhaps, the stage in the solution of this grand
difficulty which is most usually attained by thoughtful and
devout Christians. It is a conclusion in which those who
cannot help starting the inquiry, and still desire to pursue it
in the spirit of humble faith and holy reverence, may rest
with a partial satisfaction, since it reconciles, at least in
some imperfect manner, the more solemn revelations of
the Gospel with the attribute of Divine wisdom. At the
same time it remains exposed to moral and intellectual
difficulties not easily removed. For on this view every
redeemed saint must be exposed to reflections of a strange
and perplexing kind. "I might have been as happy," he
may say, "as the sinless angels, and all who are now in
misery might have shared with me this measure of felicity.
But that I might enjoy an overplus of blessing, and a
deeper insight into the Divine goodness, numbers of my
own fellows have been left to sink for ever into an abyss
of woe. And I am called upon to adore this arrangement
as the perfection of wisdom and love, and to celebrate the
infinite riches of that grace which has raised me so much
higher in glory, by the fearful price of eternal misery to
many of my fellow-sinners. How can I, without a hateful
selfishness, regard this result as preferable to the other?
Can selfishness, then, have a deeper insight into the abysses

of Divine goodness than perfect brotherly love? If this be impossible, then it must be equally incredible that creatures saved in such a way, and at such a terrible price of misery, can see further and deeper into the Divine glory than if they had been happy and holy dwellers in a sinless universe.

But the intellectual difficulty is no less formidable. The Almighty, on this hypothesis, could certainly have prevented the fall both of men and angels; but He could not bestow upon them, if unfallen, the same happiness and glory which may now be attained through the bitter experience of sin and misery. What ground of reason can there be for a double assumption, one-half of which is so plainly arbitrary? If Omnipotence forbids a limit in one direction, why not in the other? It is even harder to believe that there are heights of knowledge and happiness which the Almighty is unable to bestow on sinless creatures, who accept and desire the gift, than that moral agents, mutable though sinless, may plunge themselves into sin by their own choice, in spite of every means that can possibly be used to preserve them from a fall so terrible. In the eye of reason, the former assumption is more incredible than the latter. And since either the one or the other must be admitted as true, before we can clear the Divine wisdom and goodness, in our thoughts, from the dark cloud with which the reign of evil has obscured them, or obtain any tolerable resting place for our understandings, in gazing on the abyss of Providence, it remains to weigh the other alternative, which has perhaps never been fairly and fully examined, either by philosophers or divines.

To meet the exigency, then, of that great problem, which forces itself on our notice, in spite of ourselves, in a thousand forms, and has exercised thoughtful minds in all ages, we must advance, I conceive, a step further than Leibnitz has ventured to do, in the recognition of the unchangeable laws of being. We must enlarge still further the sphere of Omniscient Wisdom, even at the price of seeming (and it is an appearance only) to contract the range of Omnipotence. We must transfer to one Divine perfection what the darkened mind of man, seeking an excuse or palliation for his own guiltiness, has falsely referred to another, and thereby confused his own conscience, and thrown a veil of night around the ways of an all-wise Providence. We must maintain—and show the truth and consistency of the doctrine—that moral evil has neither been positively decreed, nor negatively permitted, but simply foreseen, by the God of infinite holiness, who cannot behold it without an intense abhorrence; that its entrance is an inseparable result of the creation of free moral agents; and is the object of foresight to the Omniscient Wisdom, but not of prevention even by Almighty Power; but that, having been foreseen, infinite power, wisdom, and love have conspired to provide a wonderful remedy; so that where sin hath abounded, grace will much more abound, and death shall at last be swallowed up in a glorious victory. Two main principles have thus to be established. First, that the entrance of moral evil is due entirely to the mutable will of the creature, and in no respect to the decree of the Almighty, or even to that active permission which consists in the voluntary withholding of some needful and possible succour. And, secondly, that the foresight of its first entrance, and all the awful results that have followed, are no sufficient reason why God should have forborne the highest and noblest exercise of His creative power; since evil would then have achieved a more fatal triumph, in the bare contemplation of it as possible, than now in its actual entrance and reign. The Uncreated Life would have been sealed up perpetually within its hidden fountain. God would have been defrauded of his glory, and the universe of its being.

Our first point of departure, in this difficult inquiry, must be from those facts which are already known. Men and angels are the only two races of moral agents of whose existence we have any certain information. In each instance we learn, either from revelation alone, or from revelation confirmed by daily experience, the mournful certainty of the entrance of moral evil. It is true that fertile imaginations have often busied themselves with inventing unknown races of intelligent creatures, the inhabitants of other suns or planets, among whom sin has never found a place; and have sought to gather, from beautiful dreams of their unbroken felicity, more cheerful views of the divine Benevolence, than they have thought it possible to gain from the actual history of our own world, or even from the revelations of the word of God. But these conjectures have no single grain of direct evidence. Experience teaches us nothing respecting these unknown races; and Scripture, while it reveals to us the existence of angels, both fallen and unfallen, and is rich in messages that throw light upon the ways of God, maintains on this subject a total and expressive silence. Our only safe mode of reasoning is from facts that are known, and not from the fairy dreams of imagination; which, even when most attractive on a casual glance, are apt to seduce us from the thorny ascent of truth, by which we might attain a more glorious prospect, and learn to gaze on the universe in the light of heaven. The reality, which proceeds from the Infinite Wisdom itself, could we view it in its true light, must be fairer, nobler, and more wonderfully beautiful, than all the flights of mere fancy, however captivating they may appear to be.

It is further evident that the word of God nowhere asserts what has been so often assumed by metaphysicians and divines, that the prevention of moral evil, in a world of free agents, was possible in its own nature. The fall, either of men or angels, is never ascribed, either directly or indirectly, to the will of God. Men have often added this doctrine to God's word; but they have never found it revealed. The Scriptures assume the fact, in the case of angels, and recount it, in the case of men, but without one hint that more effectual means might easily have precluded this dark apparition of evil altogether. Their most distinct revelations on this mysterious subject look rather in the opposite direction. They warn us solemnly against a dangerous delusion to which the sinner is naturally prone. "Let no man say, when he is tempted, I am tempted of God; for God cannot be tempted of evil, neither tempteth He any man." They disclaim, on the part of God, any pleasure in the continued evil of His creatures, when actually fallen. "Have I any pleasure at all that the wicked dieth, saith the Lord God, and not that he should turn from his wickedness and live?" They announce the fall of man in these expressive words: "that God made man upright, but they have sought out many inventions." And the apostasy of the first apostate, among the angels, is described in words, which still more strongly seem to discountenance the idea, that an arbitrary choice of God was a concurrent cause of his ruin. "Ye are of your father the devil, and the lust of your father ye will do. He was a murderer from the beginning, and abode not in the truth, because there is no truth in him. When he speaketh a lie, he speaketh of his own, for he is a liar, and the father of it." The Almighty Power of God is proclaimed and magnified in a thousand forms; but is never once applied to the subject before us, or asserted to include a power to have prevented altogether the entrance of evil into the moral universe.

The way is thus left entirely open, so far as the authority of Scripture is concerned, for the supposition here advanced, that the prevention of all evil, in a world of created free agents, may be strictly impossible in its own nature. We have even, perhaps, a partial presumption in its favour, since, in the two only races of moral agents whose existence is known to us, the presence and wide prevalence of moral evil is a revealed and certain truth.

There are four questions which have now to be answered, before we can determine the truth or falsehood of the supposition which has to be examined. What is the meaning of creation, in general? What are the meaning and the necessary results of creation, in the case of a free agent? What is the nature of temptation to evil, or the mutability and defectibility of the creature? And finally, what are the means, possible in their own nature, by which their apostasy could be prevented, and their continuance in holiness and happiness have been more effectually secured? What could have been done more by the all-wise Creator, for the vineyard He had planted, that He has not done? or what is there in his dealings that can warrant the notion of a voluntary and active concurrence, by way of direct permission, in the entrance of evil?

I. A view of creation has been current in the schools,

which goes far towards denying it altogether, and opens the door to a thorough Pantheism. The preservation of creatures, it is affirmed, is a continual creation. It is unfolded by Leibnitz, who adds the inferences of Bayle, and endeavours to disprove them :—

"In consequence of this doctrine, it seems that the creature never exists, that it is always being born and always dying, like time, motion, and other successive existences. Plato has believed this of material and sensible things, saying that they are in a perpetual flux, and are always *becoming*, but never *are*. But he has judged quite differently of immaterial substances, which alone he considered real; and in this he was not altogether wrong. But the continual creation respects all creatures without distinction.

"The Cartesians, after their master, seek to prove it by a principle not sufficiently conclusive. They say that the moments of time having no necessary link one with another, it does not follow, from my existing this moment, that I shall subsist the moment following, unless the same cause which gives me being now, gives it me also for the instant following. . . . . M. Weigel of Jena drew up a proof of the existence of God, which came really to this continual creation. Each moment of the existence of things depended, he said, on God, who revives everything out of himself every moment. And since they perish every moment, there needs always some one to revive them, who must be God. But this is not exact enough to be called a demonstration. It would be needful to prove that the creature is ever rising out of nothing, and falling into it again, and especially to show that the privilege of lasting more than a moment belongs by its nature to the necessary Being alone. . . . . What we may affirm with safety is, that the creature depends continually on the Divine Power, and not less after it has begun to be, than at the beginning. This dependence implies that it would not continue to exist, if God did not continue to act; and further, that this Divine activity is free. Nothing hinders but that this conservative action may be called production, and even creation. For the dependence being as great afterward as at first, the extrinsic character, of being new or not new, does not change its nature."

He then proceeds to mention the inferences of Bayle, which he himself disclaims. "We must conclude that God does everything, and that there are neither first, nor second, nor occasional causes among all his creatures, as it is easy to prove. For at this moment, when I speak, I am such as I am, with all my circumstances, such a thought, such an action, such a posture ; and if God creates me at this moment such as I am, as we must affirm on this hypothesis, He creates me with such a thought, action, motion, and determination. We cannot say that God creates me first, and then, being created, He produces with me my movements and determinations. For, since God creates me this instant, if we say that afterward He produces my actions along with me, we must of necessity conceive a second instant for this action. It is certain, then, on this hypothesis, that the creatures have no more any bond or relation with their actions than with producing themselves in the first moment of their own creation."

This doctrine, however, of the Cartesians and some scholastics, that preservation is a creation perpetually renewed, is alike opposed to Scripture and reason. It is opposed to Scripture, which speaks of creation constantly as a finished work, and puts it in contrast with the Divine government of creatures already made. For, even if we refer the seventh day and its rest to a reconstitution of our earth, rather than to the first origin of the universe, the natural conclusion from the history will be the same. The six days' creation, completed once for all, and followed by a day of rest, cannot but imply a similar contrast between the original act of creation, which called the universe out of nothing, and that ceaseless Providence which admits of no end.

The doctrine is equally opposed to sound reason. If the existences of every moment proceed immediately from God himself, and not at all from the existences of the previous moment, we have a series of perpetual illusions, a phantasmagoria momentarily produced by the Almighty, but no proper existences whatever. We have innumerable phenomena, but no beings. For continuance is essential to the very notion of a being. We may conceive of one whose duration is very short; but if it has no duration at all, it cannot possibly have a real existence. Creation, in its very nature, implies the communication of active powers to a nothing which becomes something by the very act of receiving them. It is a mysterious generation of being out of nothingness. But while acts may be momentary, powers are and must be continuous. And hence to affirm that preservation is a continual creation is really to deny a creation altogether, and plunges us into an abyss of Pantheistic darkness.

But it may be urged that the dependence of the creature on its Creator must be as complete afterward as at the beginning. This, however, is a mere fallacy. Before creation, it depends on the will of God whether or not the creature shall receive any being. After its creation, it depends on his creative will for having received those particular powers and no others. The dependence is clearly different in kind in the one state and the other. Now the moment of creation is the transition from one kind of dependence to the other; and this transition can never serve to define either kind of dependence, between which it is the transition. As soon as created, the dependence of the creature begins to be of the very same nature as it continues afterward to be; but this can never prove that it is created afresh every moment.

How, then, may creation be defined? It is the calling of a fresh existence out of nothing, by the bestowment of certain active powers, in which consist the essence and character of the new being. These powers may be perishable, if they refer to perishable objects, or include conditions of activity which cease to be fulfilled. They will be imperishable, when they have respect to indestructible objects, or to eternal and unchangeable truth. But, in either case, they are gifts of God without repentance. Creation is virtually denied altogether, when we refer all action immediately to God, and suppose a further action of his power, distinct from creation itself, to be needful for the bare continuance of all creature activity.

But does not this view interfere with the perfection of the Almighty, as the Preserver of the creatures He has made, who upholds all things by the word of his power? The reverse seems to be much nearer the truth. That cannot be preserved which has no proper existence of its own. The shifting phenomena of each moment are not preserved, but vary perpetually; and if all action were properly the action of God himself, all preservation becomes a contradiction in terms. The title is applied to Him in the Scriptures with no reference to a metaphysical idea that eludes our grasp, of a perpetually renewed creation, but with distinct relation to those creatures whose life is perishable and liable to decay, or else to that wise foresight which has ensured the continual adaptation of the material universe to the great purposes it was intended to fulfil. He " preserveth man and beast," when He so arranges all things by his Providence, that no fatal hindrance interferes with the development of their powers, and cuts short the thread of their frail being.

The creation of free agents involves a deeper mystery. The active powers bestowed are in this case the nobler endowments of self-consciousness, choice, reason, and will. Matter, in receiving active power, receives a law which it must implicitly obey. Obedience to the ordinance of the Creator is the necessity of its being. But it is not so with moral agents. The power of choice, the faculty of reason, the gift of will, imply a higher and more responsible mode of existence. Created in the image of God himself, and reflecting the spontaneity of the Divine Will, they are not his tools, but his subjects and stewards. They have a trust committed to them, and a law they are bound, but not necessitated, to obey. It is this liberty of choice, this immunity from passive and compulsory subjection to a law which enforces itself and must be fulfilled, which constitutes their peculiar dignity, as the highest and noblest of all the works of God.

The conception, however, of such a power of choice, or the free will of a moral agent, leads at once into the heart of a difficult controversy, which has tasked the intellect, and divided the judgment, of a host of meta-physicians and divines. If the will is entirely deter-mined by the circumstances in which it is placed, when combined with its own previous state, the power of choice seems to dwindle into a mere point, and free agency would be lost in a fatal necessity, as firm and unalterable as that by which water finds its level, or atoms obey the law of gravitation. If, to escape from this danger, we assume a liberty of indifference, or a power in the will to choose without a motive, like the fanciful deflexion of the atoms of Epicurus from a straight line, we intro-duce a reign of mere chance, in which all foresight is impossible. All reasoning from causes is destroyed, if innumerable events may occur continually without any assignable cause, either in the creature or the Creator; and all predictions of the future would be impossible, even to Omniscience itself. How can we escape from this perilous alternative, in which Chance and Fate threaten, each in its turn, to thrust down the living God from the throne of the universe?

To solve this hard problem, let us dwell for a moment on the conceptions we are led to form of the Divine nature. The Being of God is infinitely necessary, and yet his will is infinitely free. He cannot deny himself, but He does all things according to his own good plea-sure. This glorious antithesis, which reason itself unfolds, appears to be further illustrated in the primal mystery of the Christian faith. "As the Father hath life in himself, so hath he given to the Son to have life in himself." "To have life in himself" is equivalent to essential perfection, the necessity of unchangeable and perfect goodness. But the Father hath given this to the Son, and in the idea of a gift is involved the conception of entire freedom, and the absence of all constraint and compulsion. The necessity of being infinitely good, to speak with reverence, is the first and deepest ground of the Divine Being—the abyss where thought loses itself in pure adoration of the unsearchable. To have a free and infinite delight in all goodness, and in communicating that goodness freely, is a second aspect of the same Infinite Perfection, eternally flowing from that hidden fountain; and though equally incomprehensible in itself, is more capable of being apprehended, while it stoops to our weakness, and unveils itself in ten thousand forms of condescending love.

Now it is the very constitution of a moral and reasonable being, or free agent, to have been created in the image of God. Each of them was designed, like a dewdrop sparkling in the sunbeam, to be the reflection of his pure and perfect being. And hence the same antithesis of liberty and necessity must be found here also, as in the glorious Archetype himself. The will of such a creature is neither undetermined, which would resign the dominion of the world to chance, nor necessitated and constrained by outward circumstances, which would equally establish the supremacy of a blind and inevitable Fate. It is strictly self-determined. Circumstances and motives persuade, but do not compel. There is a real liberty, but it is not the liberty of pure indifference, or the power of deciding without any motive and reason whatever. The self which determines is the deep and hidden ground of the creature's whole being; and, as it is good or evil, decides the weight of the motives themselves, and the practical result of the circumstances out of which they arise. On the other hand, to an eye that can fathom the good and evil, actual or potential, of every

moral agent, the results of its choice will not be undetermined, but may be foreseen in the moral cause out of
which they will actually flow. This, however, can only
be attained, in all cases, by that Infinite Wisdom which
knows all the possibilities of existence, and compasses
about the very roots of all created being. That the will,
when tempted, *must* fall, is a falsehood which reason and
the word of God equally condemn. It is a choice, and not
a fatal necessity, when it does occur. That it *may* fall, is
a conclusion which might be drawn from even a partial
experience, and a limited insight into the laws of creation. That, in such and such cases, it *will* fall, is a
certain truth to the eye of Omniscience ; but the grounds
of this knowledge, except in the simpler cases of confirmed and habitual transgression, lie too deep to be
readily approached by mere human wisdom. When we
say that the will has chosen good or evil, because such was
its own character, we have gone as deep as it is possible
for us to do ; and whatever would persuade us to refer
its choice, either to the necessity of circumstances without, or a capricious, uncaused, and unaccountable impulse
within, is a falsehood which deadens the conscience,
and tends to undermine all the foundations of moral
government.

Now if such be the nature of free agency, it must
involve important consequences with regard to the mode
of the Divine operation in dealing with creatures thus
fearfully and wonderfully made. They can be dealt with
only according to the nature which the Creator has
bestowed upon them. Physical impulse and forcible
constraint are here as inapplicable as reasonings with
a stone, or expostulations with a lump of clay. So far
as we can gather, either from the voice of reason, or the

tenor of Scripture, persuasion, command, entreaty, threatening, and promise, are the only legitimate and possible modes of Divine government. A power has been given, for wise and worthy ends, the dignity of which refuses to be dealt with on lower terms ; and the Almighty would deny his own workmanship, and contradict his own wisdom, by seeking to deal with such creatures in any other way. The facts which the word of God reveals, with regard to the possible recovery of guilty and rebellious souls by Divine grace, when fairly examined, do not impeach this conclusion of reason, which finds such a mass of consenting testimony in the word of God. They do not prove that even the Almighty can change the will of man without its own consent, but only that, in certain cases, to be considered hereafter more fully, that consent may be secured. Repentance is no piece of celestial machinery, but a great and stupendous moral change. Moral agencies are always employed in producing it, though it lies deeper than the ordinary sphere of moral suasion. From the first command in Paradise, to the parting invitation, where the Spirit and the Bride say, Come, and invite the wanderers of earth to slake their thirst with the living waters of salvation, the whole of Scripture confirms the principle here advanced — that moral agents can be ruled only by moral influence ; and that mechanism, compulsion, and mere physical constraint, are means incompatible with the essential laws of their nature, which Almighty Power cannot, and Infinite Wisdom refuses to employ. And hence the supposition that such remedies can avail, when all others have failed, can be nothing else than a mischievous delusion.

CHAPTER IV.

ON TEMPTATION IN FREE AGENTS.

IT has now been endeavoured to show that the creation of free agents implies the bestowment of active powers, by which the creature is exempted from physical constraint; so that Omnipotence is self-limited, by its own gift, to deal with it in the way of moral suasion and influence alone. How far this influence may extend, in the case of a Being infinitely wise and powerful—what mighty moral engines may be brought to bear upon the spirit, or whether it may not be persuaded, by its own consent and the consciousness of need, to abdicate its own vicegerency for a season, so as to be re-created morally by a deeper work of Divine power than creation itself—are questions to be solved rather by the light of revelation and experience, than by the force of abstract reasoning. But the fundamental maxim must still be maintained, without which all Providence becomes a sea of darkness; that moral means alone are open, even to Omnipotence itself, whereby to govern a moral creation, and control the thoughts, actions, and desires of reasonable and immortal spirits, created at first in the image of God.

We have now to enter on the further inquiry—What is the nature of temptation to evil? What is that mutability and defectibility of the creature which it has been supposed that Almighty Power might hinder from passing into reality, by a simple act of the Divine will?

And, first, it seems clear that the created spirit cannot be made participant of all knowledge by a direct act of power alone. For if the creature could be thus endued by the mere volition of the Creator, it would follow that it might be at once invested with the Divine Omniscience. But an omniscient being, so far as our eyes can pierce into such mysteries, would be another God, equal to his Maker. Being infinitely wise, he must also be infinitely good, and have an infinite hatred of all evil, be infinitely happy in the knowledge of his own goodness, and infinitely remote from the possibility of being deceived, or tempted with evil. On the other hand, he must know himself to be a creature, dependent on the Creator, and debtor eternally to a goodness greater, earlier, deeper than his own. Now this appears to be an essential contradiction. God cannot create a second First Cause of all things; and for the same reason He cannot exalt a nothing, by creative power, into a second omniscience.

The communication of knowledge, then, to the rational creature, must have its laws and limits. And since God cannot be known as He is in himself, in his own unsearchableness, it seems to follow that He can be known by his words and acts exclusively—by acts of creation and messages of providence, all referred to the great unknown First Cause. These are the means by which his nature and perfections become partially known to his creatures. The Scriptures confirm this view. They tell us, that "no man hath seen God at any time: the only begotten Son, who is in the bosom of the Father, he hath revealed him." And the title under which the Son begins his revelation of the Father, is "the Word.

of God." The revelation implies a condescension, in its very nature, towards angels and men. To the former the Son appears from the first to have been manifested, as the Angel of Jehovah; and to the latter, from the hour of creation, He revealed himself apparently in a human form.

The means of knowledge, which created spirits would enjoy, must be drawn from their own consciousness, from their intercourse with spirits like themselves, and from direct revelations of God, within the limits of their creature capacity, by the great Angel of the Covenant, and their own observation of the material universe. All these rays, converging to their centre, and referred to the unknown First Cause, would constitute the earliest and primitive revelation of the Divine Being. Those moral obligations, also, which are inseparable from their nature, would be revealed to them in the shape of a Divine command, a "categorical imperative" of duty, streaming down upon them from the unknown Creator, and carrying along with it its own evidence of eternal truth. By this golden, but invisible chain, while the great law of love is obeyed, their dependent nature would remain linked with the great Source of all created being, and abide under the approving smile of the eternal King.

The temptations to evil, in such a creature, must result from the essential limitations of its own being. It is limited alike in power, wisdom, and goodness. Its will has bounds which it cannot surpass; and whether placed lower or higher among its fellows, it can easily conceive a range of activity, or a degree of authority, larger and fuller than its own. Its intellect knows something of the Maker and his works; but still more remains unknown; and it is able to speculate far and wide among these conceivable possibilities of being. It may strive in its thoughts to reconcile things incompatible, which its ignorance deems reconcilable, and thus revel amidst the seductive combinations of an ideal universe. Its goodness is limited and dependent. It continues only so long as the will abides in submission to that Divine command of love, which is its chief link of union with its Maker, and with the whole universe of being. In the observance of that law is its only safety. It is the path by which it may rise into higher and higher knowledge of the truth, and more intense activity and joy of will, in the service of the Most High, and maintain dominion over those lower creatures which He may have placed in subjection under it. But all the possibilities of good, which the intellect may conceive to lie in the undiscovered universe of being; and all the energy of the will, when it chafes, like an ocean on its shores, against the primary law of subjection that limits its independence, constitute temptations to disobedience. There is a shadowy universe of possible felicity in untried, self-chosen pathways, which arrays itself against the experience of present happiness in the service of God, and the authority of a law which commends itself, by its own light, to the deepest consciousness of the spiritual being.

Every moral agent, therefore, by the mere fact of its creation, is placed between two unknown worlds, which solicit its choice in opposite directions. It finds itself, from the first birth of inward self-consciousness, placed under a moral law, which contains its own evidence of binding obligation, but which it clearly has the power to disobey. All its actual experience, whether brief or long, has been one of happiness in obedience. But unknown regions of hope are before it. On either side the prospect is immense, of growing felicity in the tried pathway of obedience, or of conceivable happiness, higher than has yet been enjoyed, in the wider fields of independence and self-will. One road, in its first entrance, appears steep and narrow, though it leads onward and upward to the heights of celestial glory. The other is wide and facile, and seems to offer a vast range of free enjoyment, unvexed by the restraint of law, with heights and depths that appear to rival the happiness and independence of the Creator; though it leads really to a dark abyss of gloom and misery, from which only infinite wisdom and goodness, by amazing depths of condescending grace, can rescue those who have once gone astray.

Assuming, then, the creation of free agents, are there any means the Almighty has forborne to employ, by which the door might have been barred for ever against the entrance of moral evil? Could something more have been done, which He has not done, for the vineyard of immortal spirits, whether planted in the heavenly or the earthly Paradise?

There are three ways in which the opposite view may be sustained, whether it be regarded as a vindication of God's almighty power, or an imputation on his goodness. We may assume that God could have removed the sources and occasions of temptation to sin; or have abolished his own creation, the moment it was ready to fall; or have necessitated the spirit to goodness by a secret and inscrutable action of his sovereign will.

Now it is clearly within the range of Divine wisdom and power to vary the modes and forms of temptation to which his creatures are exposed. This is eminently true of man, in his present condition; but we must conceive it

to be also, though less apparently, true of pure, unfallen
spirits in heaven. But the temptation itself, apart from
its special form, arises immediately out of the very laws
and limitations of the created will; and hence its entire
removal must be simply impossible. It is the prerogative
of God alone, that He cannot be tempted with evil.
While there is an active energy of thought and will, and
a wide region of the unknown, which it has not traversed,
there must be temptation to break loose from the commands of God, and rove into those fields in search of some
higher degrees of unknown felicity. It is the province of
Divine wisdom to dispose and control the forms under
which these temptations may appear, so far as they depend, indirectly, on positive agencies; but it is equally its
province to discern that the temptation itself is the serious
and solemn ordeal which every free agent, besides God
himself, must undergo.

But might not the creature be annihilated, in the
moment when it is foreseen that temptation would prevail
against it? This suggestion is loaded with difficulties,
which make it manifestly unworthy of the Divine wisdom.
In the case of man, it would imply his destruction, almost
as soon as created, while yet sinless; and the abolition of
the whole race, without any cause that would be percepti-
ble to the rest of creation. It would replace the punishment of the sinful by the annihilation of the innocent, on
grounds cognizable by the Creator alone. In the case of
angels, the sudden extinction of those who fell, while they
were still perfect and holy, must have been a new temptation to those who were spared; leading them to regard
the Creator as a capricious despot, who delighted as much
in the destruction of the innocent as in their creation; and
might, for anything that we can tell, have been the surest

method of tempting them also into rebellion, or else have required their annihilation, to hinder a second and total apostasy of all the survivors of the first destruction. But surely it is less unworthy of the Divine wisdom to abstain from creation altogether, than to destroy all his rational creatures, almost as soon as made, and while still abiding in their uprightness, because of the foreseen strength and victory of unborn evil. It may be added, further, that the assumption itself, that a spiritual being is capable of annihilation, is liable to very grave and serious doubt, when we reflect deeply on the messages of Scripture, and the natural meaning of creation and immortality.

The third alternative is the form of the hypothesis, in which, perhaps, it finds the most general acceptance. Out of the doctrines of Divine grace the impression has arisen, and prevailed widely in the Church, that God, by a super-natural gift of grace, might have preserved men and angels infallibly in their first uprightness. We are thus taught that "because Adam had not received constancy to perse-vere, he so easily fell. If one objects that the will was placed in a slippery position, because its power was weak, it may be answered that the degree conferred was suffi-cient to take away every excuse. For surely the Deity could not be tied down to this condition, to make man such that he could not or would not sin. Such a nature might be more excellent; but to expostulate with God is more than unjust, seeing He had full right to determine how much or how little He would give. Why He did not sustain him by the virtue of perseverance is hidden in his counsel; but no necessity was laid upon God to give him more than that intermediate and even transient will, that out of man's fall He might extract materials for his own glory."

In this statement two things, widely different, are con-
founded together—what was due to man himself, and what
is consistent with the infinite perfection of Divine goodness.   I may give an alms to a beggar, who has no claim
to it; but if I let him commit suicide before my eyes,
when a single motion of my arm would have arrested the
fatal act, I should appeal in vain to the alms I had given,
in proof that I had manifested a high degree of benevolence.   In the revealed facts themselves of what the
Creator did for Adam, there is no possible ground for
impeaching his goodness.   The temptation to charge Him
foolishly arises entirely from the unproved assumption
which has been grafted on the sacred narrative, that there
was some gift, far greater and better, by which the catastrophe would easily have been averted, and which God
was unwilling to bestow.

Now this fancied necessitation of the unfallen creature
to goodness, however widely the hypothesis has been
received, appears to involve a moral contradiction.   It
must be either with or without the consent of the creature
itself.   If without its consent, it supposes God to violate
the fundamental law of the being He has just bestowed,
while it still abides in its original perfection; and to deal
with a son as with a passive lump of clay.   If with its
consent, it supposes the unfallen spirit, before any experience of evil, and in all the conscious energy of a pure and
upright will, to abdicate its own stewardship, and to anti-
cipate, by a voluntary act, the hardest and deepest results
of the stupendous economy of redeeming love.   And besides, if the creature might withdraw its consent from a
law so simple and plainly reasonable, as that which called
upon it to love its Creator with all the powers He had
bestowed, how far stronger would be the temptation to

refuse consent to a further revelation, that should call upon it to abdicate its own will, and reduce itself to a temporary state of passive impotence, in order to be thereby secured against some unknown evil of which it had no present experience? Either alternative is equally untenable in the eye of calm and sober reason; while it runs counter to the whole drift and current of Divine revelation.

A tacit appeal seems made, however, in the words just quoted from one of the first of theologians, to the experience of Christian believers, as if the assumption could be easily proved by their perseverance in the service of God. But "the virtue of perseverance" in the two instances has little in common but the name. There is a provision, in the scheme of redemption, for many a partial fall, even of believers, and many stages of recovery. The argument lies really the other way. Even in the case of His own people, whom the Lord loves with a special and distinguishing love, there can be found, in the judgment of most Christians, no example of perseverance in sinless perfection. And if this were possible, as other Christians believe, in a few cases of eminent holiness, a result so rare and exceptional, under all the richer revelations of Divine grace, is rather a presumption that the gift was entirely impossible to be imparted by any act of mere power, before the grace of redemption had dawned on the night of sin and sorrow. On every ground of reason and experience, we may well accept the conclusion that every provision was made, by the all-wise Creator, for the continued obedience of men and angels, which was consistent with the essential laws of created being; and the expostulation addressed to the rebellious Jews is equally true in its earlier and wider application to the twofold rebellion in the earthly and the heavenly Paradise. "What could have been done more to my vineyard, that I have not done to it? Wherefore, when I looked that it should bring forth grapes, brought it forth wild grapes?" Thus God will be justified in his sayings, and be clear when He is judged. His goodness and equity will be fully cleared at the last from those dark clouds, which the blasphemy of his enemies, and the dim-sighted faith of his own children, more ready to magnify his power than to apprehend the purity and perfection of his goodness, have caused to obscure the righteous providence of the Most High.

On this view, however, that the prevention of moral evil, in created free agents, is impossible in its own nature, the original difficulty appears in an altered form. Why did the Almighty exercise his creative power, in forming spirits with such lofty but perilous endowments, when He foresaw the fearful ruin into which multitudes would plunge themselves by their fall? Were it not better to have forborne a work so awful in its consequences, and rather to have sacrificed the possible happiness of the unfallen and the redeemed, than to purchase it by the foreseen misery and despair of a vast multitude, perhaps even a majority, of the creatures He has made?

There are many reasons which may be offered in reply to this objection, and some of which will come before us in the progress of the inquiry. But there is one which ought to be sufficient alone to silence every such doubt, and clear the Divine wisdom and goodness from the charge implicitly brought against them. For how can we conceive a more awful triumph of evil, than that its dark and hateful spectre, while yet unborn, should tie up the hands of the Almighty from the noblest exercise of his creative wisdom, and imprison his infinite riches of goodness within his own bosom; so that matter should never exist, because it might issue in a soulless and infinite chaos; and no reasonable souls ever spring to life, to love and adore their Creator, lest the dark power of evil should seize upon them, in spite of all his perfection, and drag them down into an abyss of ruin. To deny life to infinite numbers of holy and happy beings, whom his power could create and his wisdom govern, and in whom his goodness might delight itself for ever, through the fear of the victory of evil, in the abuse of his own gifts—what were this, but for the Supremely Good to play the coward and the murderer, and thus to deny his own being, and renounce his Godhead, lest the abusers of his free bounty should suffer the just punishment of their crimes? Must not the life, which refused to flow forth through such fears as these, at once begin to stagnate in its hidden source; and evil achieve its most fatal and awful triumph, by planting its victorious standard within the very citadel of all perfection, and turning the pure and infinite Fountain of living waters into a dull marsh, from whence no stream of goodness should ever flow? Far must it be from the Infinitely Wise thus to veil his perfect wisdom before the mere possibilities of unborn evil, and to immolate his own glory, and the being of the whole universe, on the altar of a dark and gloomy destiny. He is Light, and over Him darkness can have no power. He is the Only Good, and must do good continually with a free delight, or renounce the primal law of his holy and all-perfect being.

From these preliminary views of the nature of God, and the true source of evil, let us proceed to consider, in succession, some of the earliest acts of divine providence, that we may see more clearly the wisdom and goodness of all the counsels of the Almighty.

CHAPTER V.

ON THE CREATION AND FALL OF ANGELS.

THE first main fact of God's moral government, which the word of God reveals to us, is the creation of angels, and that subsequent rebellion by which multitudes of them became apostates from their original glory. It is a truth which looms dimly and awfully upon us through the mists of a past eternity. In the hour of creation, when the foundations of the earth were laid, these morning stars "sang together, and all the sons of God shouted for joy." But no sooner was man planted in Eden, than a mysterious Tempter appears, by whose fraud he is led astray into ruin. His names in the Scripture are descriptive of a fearful power and activity of evil. He is the Adversary of God and man, the Deceiver of the nations, the God of this world, the Prince of the power of the air, and the whole world is described by one Apostle as lying in his arms. Such descriptions must import no slight degree of power, malice, and moral influence. They open before our vision a terrible gulf, in which the noblest faculties and endowments have been fatally entombed, and lend a new emphasis to the sublime apostrophe of the prophet on the king of Babylon— "How art thou fallen from heaven, O Lucifer, son of the morning!"

To illustrate, so far as we are able, with our limited faculties, the wisdom and goodness of the Almighty in this great act of power, there are several questions to be solved, and weighty difficulties to be removed. Why did God create angels before men, when He foresaw that their fall would give birth to the temptation by which Adam fell, and which involved his posterity in moral ruin? How can it be explained that some angels have fallen, and others have continued upright, without such a recourse to the Divine Sovereignty and Omnipotence as must infer that all alike might have been sustained, and that a sinless universe is by no means a moral contradiction? Since God is infinitely good as well as holy, why do we find in his word no trace of means employed for the recovery of angels as well as men? How can we reconcile with the Divine goodness that permission of Satanic temptation, through long ages, which is clearly taught in the Holy Scriptures? Lastly, how can we reconcile the usual view of the instant punishment of evil angels, in the moment of their fall, with the fact that they are still at liberty to tempt and deceive the nations, or with the infinite long-suffering, which is one main perfection of the Almighty?

I. The creation of angels, when compared with that of mankind, has many striking features of contrast. Unlike men, they are either pure, unembodied spirits, or more probably, are clothed with ethereal bodies. Being free from the load of grosser matter, they can range throughout infinite space, and go and return like a flash of lightning, so as to visit at pleasure every region of the universe. Their knowledge as well as their power, being derived from a larger sphere, is higher than that of man. All of them have proceeded separately and immediately from the hand of the Creator, and, like Adam himself, enjoy, from the mode of their birth, the high title of sons of God. Unlike man, they neither marry, nor are given in marriage. Their being, separately bestowed, is also self-contained, and no provision is made for its diffusion, as in the human race, by celestial generations. Their number is counted by ten thousand times ten thousand, and compared to the innumerable stars of heaven; but, however vast, it is finite; and without new acts of creation, of which no hint is given us, admits of no further increase. And while the ministry of good and the temptations of evil angels, are truths clearly revealed, it is plain, from Scripture and almost universal experience, that a strict law of non-intercourse has been imposed upon them, whether by some conditions of their present being, or the direct fiat of the Almighty; so that angel visits are proverbially "few and far between," and man has very rare communications with this higher and spiritual world.

Why, then, did the creation of angels take precedence of that of man, when their fall would introduce so mighty and dangerous a Tempter, to take a leading part in the drama of human probation? Why was the Prince of fallen angels permitted to ply his seductive arts on a creature feebler and less richly endowed than himself, and thus to concur with man's own folly in plunging the new race into deep and lasting misery?

Now, first, it is plain that the character of God, as the Fountain of life, implies a free necessity, and a necessary freedom, to overflow in the production of active and sentient being. His fulness is a living fulness; and life in all its forms is never self-contained, but issues either in ceaseless activity, or in the generation of new life, which owns the former for its source and parent. Since the idea of God includes all conceivable perfection of power, wisdom, and goodness, it must include this virtual necessity of wisdom and love to call a possible universe into being.

This conclusion, it is true, may be met by a formidable difficulty. Creation cannot have existed from eternity, since a past eternity can never be actually traversed, any more than we can reach the bound of an eternity to come. But since God is from all eternity, an eternity must have elapsed before any act of creation. If He could exist so long without any creatures, why not through the second eternity, which is begun, and still in progress ? But this reasoning rests on a fundamental error. A past eternity, in succession, is only an imperfect and contradictory conception ; just as the eternity to come is not a positive fact, but an imperfect expression for that finite existence of the creature which is ever stretching onward into the infinite, but can never attain it. The being of God is one eternal Now, inconceivable to finite minds. Time began with created existence. And since the creature is not directly cognizable of God's eternity, it can only dimly reach after it, by extending its own experience into a conceivable past, and an actual or possible future. But a successive past, before creation itself, can have no real existence. "In the beginning God created the heavens and the earth." The beginning of time is the same with the act of creation. The transition, by the fiat of God, from the uncreated and infinite to finite and created being, is a real, unsearchable mystery; but a past eternity, stretching dimly backward by successive moments, years, and ages, while there was no creature in the universe, is merely a spectral, unreal image of a truth, too deep for us to comprehend in its own nature. It is the exponent of a transition from absolute, unsuccessive eternity to the actual succession of temporal things.

The certainty, then, of creation (a term which seems best to express the harmonious antithesis of freedom and necessity, where each alike is infinitely perfect) results at once from the wisdom and goodness of the Creator. Such is the view which the word of God reveals in the song of the heavenly elders—"Thou art worthy to receive honour, and glory, and power, for thou hast created all things, and for thy pleasure they are and were created." But the same reason infers that creation would not be limited to mere matter and the lowest forms of sentient life, but would include rational creatures—the noblest workmanship of the Creator's hand. If creation is a necessary inference from the perfect goodness of the Almighty, a spiritual creation is a consequence no less certainly deducible from the same truth. If all things proceed from his good pleasure, and are formed for his glory, He must eminently delight in producing immortal spirits, who wear his own image, and reflect the beauty of his own perfections; and be glorified mainly in the worship and adoration which such intelligences will rejoice to render to the great Author of their being.

But if such a creation of spiritual beings flows as a simple corollary from the perfection of the Creator, it is also natural that it should first be exhibited in its purest and simplest form. With regard to their Maker, this implies that each of them should proceed directly from his hand, so that their sense of entire dependence on his bounty may not be obscured by the intervention of any second cause. They would thus stand on the highest step of the ladder of being, and enjoy every help, accessible to the creature at first, for gazing on the uncreated Goodness. Their morning would thus be one without clouds; and, without any interposing mists of creature parentage, each of them would gaze upward on that Infinite Cause and Perfect Love, which had given them being. With regard to the universe, the same simplicity would infer that they should be bound down to no local habitation, like ourselves, but be free to visit every field of creation, and to gaze impartially, as far as thought could reach, or wing could traverse, on all the material handiworks of God. As far as we can infer from the scanty hints of revelation, this appears to be the actual constitution of the angelic world : "He maketh his angels spirits, and his ministers a flame of fire." The purest and most diffusive elements of nature are chosen to represent the condition and nature of these blessed spirits. Swiftness of wing, and the speed of wind, of fire, and of lightning—all concur in exhibiting the same truth, and set them before us, in contrast with our earthly and limited being, as real freemen of God's universe.

Such a constitution, so far as our understandings can enable us to judge, would be the most favourable to the moral stability of spiritual creatures. The links by which every one of them was consciously united to the source of his being, would be the simplest and most immediate. He would stand in the presence of his Maker, out of whose hand he had so lately come. No consciousness of earthly trammels would provoke his will to fret against the narrow limits which Providence had assigned for its action, and no temptation from the flesh could solicit its pure and sinless intelligence. A wide range over the universe would seem to give the most favourable means for apprehending the Divine glory, and escaping the delusive influence of a narrow and contracted vision. All would be favourable to stability, but, perhaps, in the same degree adverse to recovery, when once fallen. The primal sin would be more aggravated and inexcusable, and fewer means be left which the all-wise

Creator could employ, should justice allow the attempt to restore such rebels to their lost happiness and holiness again.

Now if the primal idea of Divine love be, as it certainly must be, the pure desire that His creatures, formed sinless and upright, should abide in their first estate of purity and obedience, a further reason will now appear, besides the greater simplicity of their nature, why angels should have a priority over the race of men. To borrow a significant term of some writers, the former creation has more direct reference to the antecedent, the other to the consequent will of God. In one the chief truth unfolded is the sincere will of God that his creatures should abide in that happy state in which they were created. In the other the cardinal truth is the purpose of God, in the foresight of the awful fact that rebellion will manifest itself, to exhaust the treasures of his wisdom and grace in providing a remedy. Angels were so constituted that, if it were possible, though mutable, they might stand. Man was so created, that, in the case of a fall through his own mutability, there might be the fullest concurrence of means and helps for his recovery out of that fearful ruin. And hence we may conclude that the creation of angels, earlier than man, is a signal illustration of the goodness and wisdom of the Most High, who has no pleasure in the ruin of his own creatures; and only when the mournful fact has been shown, under the most favourable circumstances for their preservation, that multitudes of them will rebel without reason, bends all the resources of his infinite wisdom, in a second creation, to provide an effectual and mighty antidote for their foreseen and anticipated crime.

II. But how shall we explain the fall of some angels,

and the steadfastness of others, without recourse to a
view of the Divine Sovereignty, which brings the clouds
of thick darkness once more over his awful countenance,
and forbids us to see in it any longer the lineaments of
a pure and perfect love? It can never be reconciled with
the instincts of natural conscience, and still less with
the tears of the Son of God, that the Almighty, because
He is almighty, should use immortal spirits as mere
counters, and, when He might glorify himself in their
universal happiness and holiness, prefer to construct out
of them a dark, tesselated mosaic of alternate holiness
and wickedness, happiness and misery. Yet if some
were maintained against temptation, why might not all
have been made to stand? If the delivering power were
in the Divine will, why was it not vouchsafed to all
equally? If in the Divine foresight alone, why were not
those alone created of whom it was foreseen that temptation to evil would be overcome?

Here we do indeed lose ourselves in deep mysteries, and need to tread softly, with holy reverence.
We cannot err on the right hand or the left, without
obscuring some Divine attribute, and either limiting
presumptuously the sovereign power of the Holy One of
Israel, or obscuring in our thoughts the pure brightness
of his eternal bounty and love. Yet, perhaps, a little
patient thought, with the help of those hints which the
Scripture supplies, will enable us to find a path through
this moral labyrinth.

The first truth, which may serve to throw light on this
obscure problem, is the Scripture statement that all the
hosts of angels were created by the Only-begotten Son
of God. "Thrones and dominions, principalities and
powers, all were created by him, and for him; and he

is before all, and by him all things consist." And since He appears in the Old Testament under the customary title of the Angel of God, we may reasonably infer that his manifestation, as the Head and Chief of all angels, is a truth of the spiritual world from the very hour of their first creation.

But the same passage, and many others, reveal to us various orders and degrees among the spirits of heaven. Archangels, thrones, dominions, princedoms, powers, and virtues, are terms which must imply a real subordination, and an ascending scale of spiritual authority. We have also mention of "the seven angels that stand in the presence of God," and of "chief princes" among the armies of heaven.

Again, there are obscure hints in Scripture, which seem to imply that Satan, before his fall, was foremost and chief among the ruling angels of the celestial hierarchy. All the descriptions of his power, and the titles given to him, as the Adversary of God, and the God of this world, would lead to the conclusion that in natural capacity he is truly the foremost of all created beings.

It is further evident, from the Scriptures, that the form of evil by which the first apostate was tempted, was pride and ambition. There was no seduction from without, or from other creatures; but his own heart was lifted up with the proud aim to rival his Creator, and set up a throne of coequal or superior dominion. Thus St. Paul, in describing the office of a bishop, gives the warning advice, "Not a novice, lest being lifted up with pride, he fall into the snare of the devil." In like manner our Lord speaks of his sin with indignation: "He was a murderer from the beginning, and abode not in the truth, because there is no truth in him. When he speaketh a lie, he speaketh of his own, for he is a liar, and the father of it." He was created, then, under a law of eternal truth, which enjoined obedience to the will of his Maker. No impulsion from without led him astray; but his own spirit, endowed with vast powers, and placed highest in the created universe, chafed against subjection to the Unseen Jehovah, as manifested in the great Angel of the Covenant, who doubtless proclaimed to all the hosts of heaven the will of the Eternal Father. But there was another infinite unknown, besides that which could be approached only through the narrow pathway of obedience to the Son of God. By abiding in the law of his creation, he seemed doubly subject to the Son of God, the visible King of heaven, and to the invisible Father, the Unsearchable, in whose name the Son claimed the allegiance of all creation. By renouncing that law, as the highest in creation besides the Son of God, and unconscious of the vast gulf which the fact of creation interposed between himself and the Uncreated Word, he might hope to be the supreme deputy and vicegerent of a second invisible and infinite, wider, vaster, and more comprehensive than the Infinite Good, which claimed his obedience. Thus pride, ambition, curiosity, and presumptuous speculation on the unknown, in contrast with the still, deep voice of conscience, propounding the eternal law of duty in obedience and love to the Creator, were the temptations which he obeyed, and thus fell irretrievably from his original glory.

This fall, like Creation itself, is an ultimate truth, and must ever remain a mystery to a finite intelligence; yet the analogy throws some light on their common but contrasted nature. In all creation there is a veiled and latent necessity, since we cannot conceive a perfect Fountain of power and goodness, without its overflowing in works and acts of beneficence. But its more prominent feature is freedom; since here is the contrast between the great I AM and every creature, that He is, because He must be, and cannot cease to be; but all other things exist, because He has freely called them into being. Now evil, viewed in its widest sense, includes the necessity which underlies the whole universe of the possible, and is a shadowy resemblance of the Divine necessity of being, with no share in the spontaneity and freedom of the Godhead. By virtue of its character, it can never touch the Divine nature; but seizes upon every created being which might possibly not have been, and attaches to it, as a metaphysical evil, from the moment of its birth, in the form of a necessary limitation, and privation of still higher modes of being. But in the form of moral evil it cannot exist, since it has nothing spontaneous or free in itself, till it has allied itself with the freedom of some positive existence. Now this can only be when the Creator, besides creating all things freely, creates moral agents endowed with his own prerogative of internal choice and freedom of will. But this marriage between metaphysical evil, which is necessary, and the free-will of the creature, out of which is born moral evil, must remain a mystery different in kind, yet very similar, to the mystery of the Divine Existence. We conceive that the Being of God is necessary, and that his will is perfectly free, and that these contrasts, in Him, must have an eternal harmony, though the mode surpasses our understanding. In like manner moral evil implies a similar union between the eternal necessities of all creature existence and the freedom of moral agents; but of this union, unlike the other, we can merely perceive by reasoning that it is necessarily possible, while the fact is proved by experience. But how the transition is made by which the necessarily possible becomes actual, without such a ground of foresight as shall make it simply a necessity, and thereby alter its essential character from a moral to a purely natural evil, is perhaps almost as inconceivable to our minds as the infinitude and necessary freedom of the Divine nature itself. We can only recognise the solemn fact, and pause with reverence on the threshold of the Infinite and the Unknown.

Still, without pretending to solve this deep mystery, the thought must naturally suggest itself, that it was the actual primacy of the first apostate which proved the special occasion of his fall. Our great poet seems here, as in several other points, to have mixed the truest and deepest philosophy with his flights of creative imagination, when he thus portrays the supposed reflections of the lost archangel :

> " Lifted up so high,
> I 'sdeigned subjection, and thought one step higher
> Would set me highest, and in a moment quit
> The debt immense of endless gratitude,
> So burdensome, still paying, still to owe."

It is true that this lofty position would give a deeper intensity to the voice of conscience, when it claimed unequalled gratitude for gifts unequalled through the wide range of created things. But the temptation to aspire still higher, and break loose from the one law which alone seemed to place him below the Son of God, seems, by the sad and awful fact, to have grown in a more than equal degree, with the vastness of the obligation. And if this be true, it seems to follow that the foresight of such a catastrophe was involved in the very fact of a spiritual creation, and would not have been altered by any con-

ccivable arrangements in the varied powers, numbers, and
constitution of the celestial hierarchy.

But when once the Fall had become an awful fact, in
the person of the chief apostate, the Father of lies, the
moral conflict, in every other instance, would inevitably
assume new features. A spirit endued with the largest
powers bestowed upon any creature, would seem, to all
inferior spirits, apart from the great moral distinction of
good and evil, a complete rival to all that they could
know and apprehend of the Most High, when self-humbled
in the person of the Word, to meet the range of their
limited understanding. This great rival, by his own disobedience, would now be able to wield all the manifold
possibilities of evil, in seductive hopes, and racking and
terrible fears, and gloomy suspicions of the Divine goodness, which the infinite abyss of the unknown could
supply. There would be fresh and endless engines of
temptation, when this dark void of all possible and conceivable evil, of which the Scripture name is DEATH, had
gained a living and actual vicegerent, its lord and slave
at once, the Prince of evil, who hath the power of death.
And there would also now be room for fresh revelations
of the Only Good, founded on this sad experience of the
creature's mutability, and the awful disclosure of spiritual
wickedness. With such rival powers, each nearly equal
in apparent, visible potency, and each alike reposing on a
secret, infinite necessity, that might seem, because unknown, equally firm, powerful, and boundless on either
side, so that only the Omniscient Eye could discern the
immense contrast between them; it is quite conceivable
that the preservation of the whole universe of spirits may
have been, to the same Omniscience, a clearly discerned
impossibility; while his power and wisdom, by the secret

disposal of His All-wise Providence, might secure the preservation of the holy angels when the others fell. The
patent and obvious source of this great contrast is the free
choice of the righteous ones to abide in the truth of God,
and the free choice of the apostates to renounce their
allegiance, and, in league with the Arch Apostate, to
plunge boldly, in search of a higher felicity, into all the
unknown possibilities of a rebellious freedom. But the
result, in each case, may be so really shut in by the secret
disposal of the wise Creator, that the holy may be truly
styled the elect angels, and ascribe to the Lord their own
continued steadfastness of will in the narrow pathway of
sinless and unswerving obedience.

The fall of angels, we may infer from the united
voice of reason and revelation, consisted essentially in
a double crime of the intellect and the will. In the
intellect, it was the renunciation of a known truth, embodied in the great law of obedience, and commending
itself by its own light to the pure consciousness of the
spirit, for a phantom of boundless happiness in the wide
regions of the unknown, to be attained by the awful
experiment of disobedience. In the will, it was the
ambitious pride which affected rivalry with God, and
ungratefully repaid the richest and noblest gifts of His
love, by seeking to turn them into engines for supplanting
his authority, and thereby set up a mightier empire of
evil over the intelligent universe. Hence it is described
under these two essential characters, in the word of God,
as an object of intense and perfect abhorrence to the
Holy One. We are told of the great Adversary, that " he
was a murderer from the beginning, and abode not in
the truth, because there is no truth in him;" while his
crime, and its final result, are described in the vivid

B.   F language of the prophet: "Thou hast said in thine heart, I will set my throne above the stars of God; I will sit in the mount of the congregation, in the sides of the north; I will ascend above the height of the clouds; I will be like the Most High. Yet thou shalt be brought down to hell, to the sides of the abyss." That one great act of sin enclosed in its womb every variety of hateful wickedness, with every fruit of awful misery that would desolate the universe, and make some of its fairest portions, for long ages, like a howling wilderness of sin and sorrow.

III.   But however deep and awful the crime of the apostate angels, there is something which seems almost to grate upon the instincts of the Christian heart in the popular view of their instant and overwhelming punishment.   How shall we account for the notorious fact that in the work of our great poet, such an unwilling interest, sometimes amounting to a conscious sympathy, is often felt, in spite of the purpose of the writer and instincts of the reader, for the great Author of evil?   In the description of the crime itself, and its probable occasion and character, Milton has kept very close to the intimations dimly scattered through the word of God.   Is it clear that this is equally true with regard to the sentence on the fallen spirits; and that there was really, in their case, no exhibition whatever of God's infinite long-suffering?   This is a weighty inquiry.   And perhaps it will be found that the instinctive feeling alluded to betrays a wide departure, in the popular impressions which the poet has adopted, from the real facts of Divine Providence; and that, instead of trembling at the spectacle of a justice awfully severe, with no trace of patience and long-suffering, we ought rather to adore a depth of forbearance towards the most aggravated and wicked abuse of mercies, that will fill the redeemed with awe and wonder through the ages of the world to come.

The view which has long been current in popular theology, that the Great Adversary and his angels were instantly cast down from heaven into the lowest pit of hell, and there tormented with fiery judgment, is chiefly founded on two passages of the word of God—2 Pet. ii. 4; Jude 6, 7. But these are very far from bearing the weight of so vast an inference. Angels, in both cases, are mentioned indefinitely; so that the words do not apply, by any necessary construction, to all the angels who have sinned. And besides, while both passages evidently refer to the same event, the second, in its further mention of the cities of the plain, affirms the sin of these angels to have been some form of unnatural lust. Accordingly, in the early times of the Church, they were usually applied to the event in Gen. vi. 2, 4, and viewed as a fuller statement of the sin of the sons of God, with its deserved punishment. This view of the meaning has been revived in modern times, and is supported by the simplest laws of criticism, in one of the passages, while it agrees with all the other features of the sacred text. It will follow that this was a second, and not a first, angelic apostasy; and because of the unnaturalness of the crime, and its more external and visible character, was visited with instant judgment.

This difficulty being once removed, the whole evidence of Scripture will point, in perfect harmony, to a view of God's dealings towards the fallen angels, widely different from that which has been popularly received, and which the sublime fancy of Milton has almost rendered, with many, a part of their habitual faith. The clearest light thrown on the subject in the Old Testament, is in the

books of Job and Daniel. In the former Satan appears
as one who ranges at liberty through the whole earth, and
presents himself boldly in heaven amongst the sons of God.
In the latter we have mention of chief princes among the
angels, with whom the Angel of the Covenant sustains a
prolonged and balanced conflict, and only one of the angel-
princes is said to be on his side in the celestial warfare.
In Zechariah we have a vision, where Satan appears before
the Angel Jehovah, to resist openly the exercise of His
grace towards Jerusalem, and, instead of instant judgment,
he hears only a prayer significant of his future doom:
"The Lord rebuke thee." In the New Testament he meets
us first as the Tempter of our Lord, with the boastful
profession on his lips that he has power over all the king-
doms of the earth, and their glory, and gives them to whom
he will. This is not the language of a criminal who is
undergoing already a most terrible and crushing sentence.
All the sorrows and diseases which our Lord relieved and
healed, are ascribed to his wicked and malicious activity:
"He healed all that were oppressed with the devil." Our
Saviour styles him "the Prince of this world," and speaks
of his casting down as the future result of His own wonderful sacrifice. The same truth he describes elsewhere,
in these expressive words,—"I beheld Satan as lightning
fall from heaven." And the whole context proves that
this denotes a future triumph, to be achieved through that
preaching of the Gospel which had just begun, and does
not describe an event far away backward in the records of
eternity. In like manner, St Paul refers every hindrance
thrown in his path to the agency of this mighty enemy.
He calls him the God of this world, the Prince of the
power of the air, the Spirit who energizes in the children
of disobedience, whose overthrow is not an accomplished

fact, but a hope of the true Church of Christ in days to come. St Peter describes him, in similar language, as free and active in his works of malice, a roaring lion, loose and bent upon his prey—not caged and fettered, or sunk in a gloomy dungeon of despair. St John tells us, with reference to the extent of his power, that the whole world, in his days, was lying in the arms of the Wicked One. In another place we are reminded that the conflict of the Christian warrior is "not against flesh and blood, but against principalities and powers, the rulers of the darkness of this world, and spiritual wickednesses in heavenly places." Finally, in the latest message of the Spirit of God, three stages of the overthrow of Satan are revealed. In the first he is cast down from heaven to earth. In the second he is chained in the abyss, to deceive the nations no more. In the third and last he is consigned to his final punishment. But all alike, from the first to the last, are events which were still future when the prophecy was given.

In reality, the doctrine which has been enshrined in glorious poetry, and embodied in treatises of theology, till it has become almost like an article of Christian faith, that instant and terrible judgment was inflicted at once upon the fallen angels, and that they were loosed afterward to become the tempters of mankind, is hard to reconcile with the moral instincts of a spiritual mind, or with any just and true conceptions of the infinite wisdom and goodness of the Almighty. We may conceive, however solemn and fearful, an instant and irreversible judgment to fall upon rebel angels in the very hour of their enormous crime; and that the severity of the Divine justice might thus be shown, without mixture of long-suffering. Or we may conceive of a continued and wondrous forbearance, until the measure of their guilt was full, and new crimes against mankind had redoubled the blackness of their first apostasy from the will of God. But this alternation of terrible punishment, suspended to give an opening for fresh crimes, does violence to the fundamental notions of equity and wisdom in a moral government. What should we think of an earthly sovereign who should loose convicted murderers, under sentence of death, in whom there was no trace of penitence, that they might be the occasion of tempting other subjects, still comparatively or entirely innocent, to become sharers in their guilt, so that the executioner at last might have a double harvest of blood? But if the thought would revolt us in the dealings of an earthly ruler, what is there, in the Almighty Power of God, to erase these moral outlines, which His own hand has engraven upon the consciences of men? "Far be it from God, that he should do wickedness; and from the Almighty, that he should commit iniquity." The conception of sovereignty must have grievously overshadowed those of infinite goodness and wisdom, before we can accept such a view of God's dealings with rebellious angels, when it departs so widely from the inference that flows naturally from all the consenting testimony of the word of God.

The further questions which grow out of this mysterious subject would be more conveniently examined in a further stage of the inquiry. For the present, we may receive provisionally a view of God's Providence towards the fallen angels, in which justice has been hitherto less conspicuous than infinite patience and long-suffering. The subtlety of evil is no less awful than its desperate wickedness; and in the person of the Great Adversary, whose first name is the Serpent, aspires to rival the wisdom of the Creator.

If Judas remained long undetected among the twelve Apostles, it is conceivable that the crime of the Arch-deceiver may have remained concealed for a time, except from the eye of the Omniscient alone. We may conceive that the Adversary was still permitted to appear among the sons of God, and to seek, in the courts of heaven itself, to veil his dark malice under the show of a zeal for the Divine justice, and his fraudulent temptations under the specious show of genuine benevolence towards angels and men. We may conceive, further, that one main object of God's Providence in the creation and redemption of mankind may be to unmask all these subtleties of wickedness in the heavenly places, to expose the frauds of the Great Deceiver and his accomplices in their true colours, and only to execute upon them their righteous sentence, when the quiver of their deceits has been exhausted, and the awful consequences of their malice have been fully displayed. Thus hell from beneath will be moved to meet this King of Babylon in his final downfall; and not only the saved, who have been rescued by Divine grace, but the lost who see in Him the Destroyer who has effected their ruin, will own the awful righteousness of the Supremely Good and Holy, when this Deceiver of this universe is crushed under the victorious feet of the once crucified and now exalted Son of God.

CHAPTER VI.

ON THE CREATION AND FALL OF MAN.

THE moral difficulties connected with the Fall of man come nearer home to the heart and conscience of mankind than those which refer to the history of angels. Self-love takes occasion, from the depth and obscurity of the Divine counsels, to awaken doubts, fears, suspicions, and questionings, which lead, in too many instances, to open blasphemy. Christian divines themselves have not been altogether blameless in this matter. They have had a zeal for God, but not always according to knowledge. Too often a sincere desire to maintain the authority of Scripture has been separated from a loving and humble spirit. In this case the sin of the Pharisees, with respect to the ceremonies of the law, has been transferred to the deeper mysteries of the Gospel; and heavy burdens, grievous to be borne, have been laid upon the natural conscience, which the imposers have not cared to lighten with one of their fingers. A strange notion seems almost to have been entertained, that faith was magnified, in proportion as the truths of revelation were presented in a shape repulsive to the moral instincts of thoughtful men. When conscience has been disposed to revolt against the burden, it has been sought to silence it by an appeal to the authority of the Bible,

without any answering efforts to enlighten it on the ways
of Divine Providence. The great Enemy of souls has
seized the advantage given him by a misdirected cham-
pionship of truth. Objections have been dressed up in
their most seductive and specious form: and distortions or
exaggerations of revealed truth, in the writings of pious
men, have been used to allure men away from the God of
the Bible, whose character has been clothed in austere and
gloomy colours; so as to transfer their worship to an
imaginary Deity, who is satisfied with a vague, dreamy,
sentimental religion, and who is supposed to be gifted with
a more diffusive and all-embracing benevolence.

The history of the Fall, after being obscured by the
additions or comments of human theology, and further disguised by the mists of the carnal heart, has been one frequent source of these infidel illusions. The thrice Holy One
has been boldly defamed and maligned as a monster of reck-
less cruelty. Can we believe, it is asked, that the God of
love should forbid the eating of an apple to our first
parents for no reason but to prove his own authority; and
then, for so slight a transgression, should condemn countless millions of their posterity, who never saw or tasted the
forbidden tree, to eternal and infinite torment in the
flames of hell? Can such a picture of Divine Providence
be reconciled with any just views of infinite benevolence?
If such are the first lessons of the Old Testament, must we
not cast it aside as a superstition unfit for an age of light;
and adopt a purer and gentler creed from modern science,
which looks through Nature up to Nature's God, and
adores, in sun and plant and flower, a benevolent Deity,
who is preparing all His creatures alike for a felicity
without end?

There are several great questions which need to be

answered, before the mists which have gathered round the history of the Fall can be cleared away, and disclose to us, in the wisdom and goodness of the Creator, a landscape fairer than that of Paradise. Why was man created, flesh as well as spirit, since a new source of temptation was hereby added to those purely spiritual delusions which had proved so fatally potent in the angels that fell ? Why were the whole race created in Adam, as the common stock and root of their being, instead of being formed separately, like Adam and the holy angels, since it was also foreseen that their common head and parent would fall, before their own separate existence had begun ? Why was the tree of knowledge of good and evil planted in Paradise within reach of man, and then forbidden to be tasted, instead of every prohibition being removed, and the tree of life alone set before him, with its precious boon of immortality? Why was woman given to be a helpmeet, when it was known that her greater weakness would expose her more easily to temptation, and smooth the descent for man into a precipice of ruin ? Why was so mighty a Tempter permitted to ply his seductive arts upon creatures weaker than himself, who proved unequal to contend with his sagacious wickedness, and fell at once into the snare he had woven for their destruction ? Why were the consequences of the Fall made to extend to unborn millions, who had never tasted of the forbidden tree ? If by positive and arbitrary appointment, why was a covenant made, that seems to trench on the laws of distributive justice ? If by a natural and necessary consequence, how could that original constitution of human nature be good and wise, which made the moral corruption and guilt of untold millions the necessary fruit of one brief and solitary act of individual transgression ?

Now it is not enough to say that the facts are revealed, and that God is just and holy, good and wise, and therefore all further inquiry is presumptuous and dangerous. The conscience of man is too mighty a power to be set at rest by theological evasions. We may not, without folly, expect in this life to see all the reasons of the Divine counsels. But when we build up laboriously a human system on the basis of revealed facts, we are bound to require that the results shall not clash violently with the consenting voice of Scripture and reason concerning the fundamental attributes of the Most High. We are not at liberty to call that conduct justice and wisdom in the Almighty, which we should charge with folly or cruelty in a human governor, nor to silence doubts, which may have arisen from our own unskilful handling of the word of life, by a bare appeal to the Divine Sovereignty, as if the Most High were exalted above those eternal laws of justice and goodness which are binding on all the reasonable creatures He has made. This is nothing else than that sin of accepting persons, which the God of truth and holiness has so sternly and repeatedly condemned. Such erring advocates of Divine truth, however sincere in their mischievous course, must expect to hear from Him the reproof which Job addressed to his friends—" Will ye speak wickedly for God ? and talk deceitfully for Him ? Will ye accept persons ? will ye contend for God ? Is it good that He should search you out ? He will surely reprove you, if ye do secretly accept persons." We may and ought to acquiesce humbly in the justice and wisdom of his ways, when we cannot comprehend them. But we ought not to be guilty of the presumption of claiming to manifest their justice by principles, which we should discard at once as injustice or folly, when applied to the conduct of earthly sovereigns. By a reverent and humble search into Scripture, we may gain some light, even here, upon the wisdom of His holy Providence. But if our dim vision leaves us still in twilight, or almost in darkness, let us beware that we never confound the dark spectres that flit before our eyes, and which will be dispelled by one glimpse of the Sovereign Goodness, with the real lineaments of the Only Good and the Supremely Wise. Clouds and darkness may now be round about Him; but of this we may have full assurance, that justice and judgment are the strong and eternal foundations of His throne.

I. Let us first inquire, with humility, why man was created with a nature so different from that of angels, and constituted with an earthly body, which would be the inlet of a new variety of temptations? Why was he fashioned of the dust of the ground, instead of being formed, like celestial spirits, by a pure act of creative power, and with a purely spiritual being?

That the constitution of human nature does open a wider range for temptations to evil, is not only the voice of natural reason, but seems directly asserted in the word of God. Such is, perhaps, the true sense of that passage in Gen. vi. which has caused so much discussion—"My Spirit shall not always strive with man, for that he is flesh also; yet his days shall be a hundred and twenty years." A contrast is here implied between some creatures, who were spirit only, and punished at once, and man, who was flesh as well as spirit, and should therefore have a long reprieve from deserved judgment. The sons of God, mentioned just before, are thus implied to have been angels, that had been guilty of crime unnatural and doubly inexcusable, from their spiritual nature; and for whom there had been no such reprieve, as for the sinners of mankind. But this plainly teaches that man's bodily constitution, in the eye of the righteous Judge, was the inlet of strong temptations, which would not have equally assailed a purely spiritual being. Why, then, was he created still more exposed to temptation than the angels themselves before their fall?

The real key to this difficulty seems to consist in that fundamental contrast which has been hinted before. While all the attributes of Jehovah abide in perfect harmony in His own infinite being, in His acts of Providence they have each to be separately displayed— never in complete isolation, but still with an alternate predominance of Divine glory. The key-note in the constitution of angels is the pure delight of God in the sinless perfection of his reasonable creatures. He has made all things for his own glory; but it is the glory of unselfishness. He, the Infinitely Good, does not seek that his creatures should fall, that his purity may shine the brighter by their guilt, and his blessedness by the darkness of their misery. The selfish and cold-hearted might, perhaps, if invested with almightiness, aim to illustrate their own perfection by laying snares and pit-falls for the blind, and planning temptations for the weak and mutable; but far be such thoughts from the God and Father of our Lord Jesus, who shed tears of grief over the sin of Jerusalem. And hence, in the creation of angels, all things were disposed with a view to their continued stability; as if the Holy One, having blessed them so highly, and gifted them with a being so closely resembling his own, with no external inlet of temptation, would not even contemplate the possibility of their wicked rebellion against the bountiful Creator. But when the truth, already known to his Omniscience, had become a mournful fact in the eyes of the universe, the God of truth recognises the mutability of the creature in all the arrangements of a second creation. The key-note, in the formation of man, is no longer sinless and unfallen perfection, but the possibility of redemption out of a fall distinctly foreseen. Seen in this light, what might else appear dark and perplexing becomes lit up with a mysterious beauty of Divine love. With the entrance of sin redemption begins its course ; and the voice of mercy, pointing to the promised Seed of the Woman, takes precedence of the sentence which banished the guilty sinner from the Paradise of God.

Now there are two great facts which meet our eye in the word of God, and throw light on the present diffi-culty. The first is that no hint is ever given of redemp-tion, as either actual or possible, in the case of pure spirits, who have once left their own habitation and departed from their God. It is certainly conceivable that their recovery may be possible in its own nature, but that the holiness of God, from the aggravated nature of their rebellion, may choose to deny them the succours of his grace. Yet, when we remember the riches of his mercy in the most aggravated forms of human iniquity, we may well incline to the other view, that his holiness simply acquiesces, with infinite consent, in a solemn fact, which his Omniscience may recognise, that for such creatures there is no possible remedy.

Secondly, it is equally clear that the whole economy of man's redemption rests entirely upon the duality of his being. The central fact on which it depends is thus announced : "The Word was made flesh, and dwelt among us." "Forasmuch as the children are partakers

of flesh and blood, he himself likewise took part of the
same, that through death he might destroy him that
had the power of death, that is, the devil ; and deliver
those who, through fear of death, were all their lifetime
subject to bondage. For verily he took not on him
the nature of angels, but he took on him the seed of
Abraham." "God, sending his Son in the likeness of
sinful flesh, and for sin, condemned sin in the flesh." In
these and other passages, the whole gist of redemption
is made to turn on the assumption of flesh by the Son
of God, whereby the Just and Holy One had a link of
natural unity with the fallen and sinful, and laid hold
upon the lost, to raise them into holiness again. Whether
we reflect upon the objective work of our Lord in his
atoning sacrifice, or the subjective application in the
moral power of his cross and resurrection, the same
truth is equally conspicuous. It is through that element
of man's nature which he does not share with angels,
and which at first made him more open to the wiles of
the Tempter, that alone he has the blessed hope of recovery out of his ruin into the image of the incarnate
Son of God.

It is in full agreement with the same idea, that the
whole course of this recovery, in every righteous man, is
described as a perpetual conflict of the flesh and the
spirit, in which the flesh is tamed, subdued, mortified,
and abolished, that the spirit may be renewed day by
day; till at length the redeemed spirit receives back
the body, no longer fleshly, but spiritual and glorious,
to be its garment of light and praise for ever. And
hence we may safely infer, that man was created
with a twofold nature, although the inlets of temptation were hereby increased, because in this way alone

his redemption was possible, and the Redeemer could unite himself with a fallen race, and bear up, with almighty grace, the sinking pillars of the moral universe.

Viewed in this light, as a provision for a future redemption, the wisdom of the Divine workmanship stands out in striking and bold relief. Pride was the sin by which angels had fallen, and would continue the grand snare to entangle and ruin the souls of fallen men. What remedy, simply of a moral nature, could tend more powerfully to their recovery, than the consciousness of being formed out of the dust, and the spectacle, daily before their eyes, of the sinner turning to dust again? The first sentence was a deep moral lesson, no less than a just punishment of sin,—"In the sweat of thy face thou shalt eat bread, until thou return unto the earth, for out of it thou wast taken; for dust thou art, and to dust thou shalt return." There is thus a deep emphasis in the phrase of the Apostle, where he calls the human frame "the body of our humiliation." It is, since the Fall, the most universal sacrament and standing ordinance of the Most High, by which He stains the pride of all glory, and brings into contempt all the honourable of the earth. Heathen moralists, in a thousand forms, have taken up this humbling message.

> "Hi motus animorum atque hæc discrimina tanta
> Pulveris exigui jactu compressa quiescunt."

" His breath goeth forth, he turneth to his dust, in that very day his thoughts perish." Earth to earth, ashes to ashes, dust to dust, is a voice resounding in the ears of each passing generation, to reclaim the prodigals from their pride, and bring them back, in lowly penitence, to the footstool of Divine mercy.

II. But, assuming this twofold constitution of man's nature, why were the whole race created in one common root, out of which innumerable multitudes were to proceed, when it was foreseen that their first parent would fall from his original righteousness, and thereby involve them in his own ruin?

Now it is plain that the reply to this question, to be complete, must involve a decision on the degree of responsibility which attaches to the children of Adam for the sin of their first parent, and the extent to which they are personally implicated in the effects of his original crime. This subject is so important, that it will require a separate discussion. At present, there are a few more general remarks, which will furnish a partial explication of this new principle of the Divine economy.

And first, it may be observed that there has been a tendency, in some modern divines, to draw a strong contrast between the parental and the federal character of Adam. They conceive that specific blessings were promised him, by a special covenant as the head of a whole race, and that these chartered gifts alone were forfeited by the whole race upon his transgression. This covenant of works, made with our first parent, has been sometimes drawn out with all the details of a legal document, in the contracting parties, the conditions prescribed—the promise of eternal life upon perfect obedience, and the punishment of eternal death upon disobedience, to Adam himself, and his whole race. But this large superstructure, whatever portion of truth it may contain, rests upon a very narrow foundation. This notion of an artificial covenant, and the broad distinction between the federal and the parental character, have no warrant at all on the face of the sacred narrative. There is much reason to fear lest, by additions of our own, we should merely darken the counsel of God, and increase the real perplexity of the subject by every element of a purely arbitrary and positive kind, which we introduce for the sake of a fancied symmetry. The word covenant is never applied to this constitution in Paradise, though Israel's transgression of the Sinai covenant is once compared to Adam's original breach of the Divine law. And the word itself does not include, of necessity, the idea of a mutual agreement, founded on the deliberate consent of two parties, but is applied to any law or promise which proceeds simply from the will of the Divine Lawgiver. No trace, also, can be found in the narrative, of a contrast between the parental and federal character. On the contrary, every effect of Adam's sin upon his posterity is clearly described as resulting from the laws of human generation. The sacred text evidently gives no hint of a specific term of probation, to be followed by the reward of a higher happiness. There is an implied promise of continuance in his actual felicity, during his obedience, with a threatening of death from the first moment he should disobey. Nor can any trace be found of a distinct and positive stipulation, affecting his posterity. They would, by the original law of his creation, have been born like their parent, had he continued upright and holy; and after his fall, they are simply described as being still born in the likeness of their father. The only elements of the moral problem, in which sovereignty appears, are the original constitution of human nature, and the solitary prohibition and warning. All besides is described as the natural result of obedience on one side, or of disobedience on the other.

There are several objects, directly secured by this new constitution of human nature, if the difficulty can be removed, which relates to the equity of God in dealing with every individual of the race. In the first place, the creative power of the Almighty was exceedingly glorified by this new gift bestowed upon man, to be the parent of reasonable creatures, born in the image of God; so as to reflect, in a way unknown to angels, the living perfection of his Creator, who is the Fountain of life and reason to the whole universe. In the next place, there was a provision in this new arrangement, if so it pleased the bountiful Creator, without any fresh act of new creation, for a perpetual increase of holy worshippers of God; so that the infinitude of the Divine nature, absolute and complete in itself, might be imagined in this relative infinitude of man's nature, which was created capable of unfolding, enlarging, and multiplying without end, through the course of innumerable generations. There was, further, a new and variegated bond of love, by which the different members of the new race might be united to each other; and parental, conjugal, filial, and brotherly affections, in immense varieties of goodness, might diversify the simplicity of creature love, which had been previously unfolded in the fellowship of the holy angels in heaven. The Apostle tells us that principalities and powers in heavenly places learn, through the Church, the many-varied wisdom of God. And certainly, apart from the deeper wonders of redemption, there were capacities of blessedness, and new capabilities of loving and being loved, in man's original law of being, the view of which might alone account for the gladness of that hour when "the morning stars sang together, and all the sons of God shouted for joy."

Even in the prospect of the Fall, which quickly marred this beautiful landscape of hope and praise, two great ends were plainly fulfilled by the same mysterious arrangement. The mournful lesson of mutability and corruption, and the bright hope and promise of redemption, were made at once objective truths to the whole race. Each member of it would enter upon his separate probation, with the dark shadow of a common calamity around and behind him, and a common hope held out, like a bow of promise, before him. He would thus be taught practically, from the first rise of a personal consciousness of sin, the threefold lesson of humiliation for a fallen estate, of dependence on the promise of God for a possible restoration, and of brotherly sympathy with all men; since they are seen to be involved along with ourselves in one common fall, and are visited alike, by the mercy of God, with the invitations and promises of one wide and glorious redemption.

III. Another main difficulty, which has given occasion to unbelieving spirits for questioning the wisdom and goodness of God, is found in the probation imposed on Adam, and the narrative of the threatening connected with the Tree of Knowledge. The usual explanations of Christian divines go a little way, and only a little way, towards removing this perplexity. It is true that God, as the Supreme Sovereign, must have had full right to impose conditions upon his own creatures, and to require obedience to his own command. It is further true that the insignificance of the forbidden object would rather aggravate, than excuse, wilful transgression of the Divine command. But a harder question remains,—how far it consists with the perfect benevolence of God, no less than with his justice, to have planted this tree in Paradise; and after thus exposing his own creature to a real temptation, to suffer the entrance of a most subtle Tempter, who would ply all his art, only too successfully, to mar the beauty of God's works, by deceiving Man their new lord, and in the person of our first parents destroy at once the whole race of mankind.

The name of the tree itself has been found not easy to explain. Some interpret by the foreseen event, that the knowledge of good would be acquired by losing it; and that of evil, by experiencing it. Others refer it to the Lawgiver, who would test by this tree whether his subject would be morally good or evil. Others expound it, "the tree of prudence," because the faculty of prudence was to be signally exercised by means of it. But it may well be doubted whether any of these offers the true key to its meaning. On the first view it should rather be called, "the tree of the knowledge of evil," since only good was experienced before tasting it, and only evil afterwards. The second view is still more unnatural, since the phrase clearly refers to Adam and Eve, and not to the Almighty. The third view agrees very ill, either with the form of the temptation, or with the words of God, when Adam was expelled from Paradise—"Behold, the man is become as one of us, to know good and evil." For although these are often stated to be a solemn irony, a comparison with the previous statements, Gen. ii. 9, 17, iii. 5, 6, 7, will at least render it very doubtful whether this can be the true and full meaning.

Let us now inquire whether a careful comparison of revealed truths will not reflect a fuller light on this affecting narrative, and do much to clear away the mists which have been thrown up, from the evil heart of unbelief, to obscure the wisdom and goodness of the Creator in this first main act of Providence towards the race of mankind.

Now if we assume, as appears to have been often done, that this avenue of temptation was arbitrarily introduced by the Almighty Creator for the mere pleasure of displaying his own sovereignty, and that the dreadful sentence was affixed in the same arbitrary manner, including the fearful doom of eternal misery; we may, by an effort of faith, adore the Divine justice in this arrangement, but it must seem strangely isolated from the sister perfection of a full and perfect benevolence. And if we further assume that the guilt of this act, by the same arbitrary decree of God, or even by the consent of Adam, ignorant of what the promise involved, was extended to the infants of all coming generations, and brought them under a sentence of everlasting misery, it is difficult not to feel the doctrine to be wholly at variance with our conceptions of the Divine justice itself. And it does not relieve the difficulty, to speak of the rich grace manifested in redemption. For unless the original sentence reveal the lineaments of a spotless equity, no later acts of grace can remove the imputation on the Divine government. Grace loses its very nature, if it needs to be resorted to, in order to vindicate the justice and equity of the sentence for which it provides a remedy. All doubts respecting the wisdom, equity, and goodness of the Almighty, in the history of the Fall, must paralyse the moral power of the Gospel, and rob that celestial message of all the brightness of its glory.

But there is no need that these dark clouds should be suffered to obscure our view of the Divine goodness in this original dispensation to mankind. For, in the first place, it is clear that the presence or absence of temptation did not depend simply on the presence of the tree of knowledge. Angels had sinned and fallen, without any such visible test; and it was equally possible that man might copy the sad example of their rebellion. The law of obedience and love was essential, in its very nature, to man's felicity; and its transgression through pride and ambition, without any visible symbol, would equally have plunged him into a gulf of moral darkness. The way of life and of death was before him by the very fact of his moral and spiritual being; and the reality of his probation did not depend on any arbitrary choice or volition of his Creator. Divine Omniscience knew the solemn fact; Divine Omnipotence did not call it into being. It followed, as an inseparable shadow, on that gift of free agency, by which man, like angels, was created in the image of God.

The same probation, through which the angels were still passing, and by which so many principalities in heavenly places had fallen, was inseparable from the moral being of man. It only remained open to the Divine goodness to diminish its perils, and contract the danger within the narrowest compass. The strength of the snare depended mainly on the ignorance of the creature, whose narrow understanding was placed between two vast unknowns, of which the good appeared to have a narrow and steep entrance, and the evil a wide and easy access; since the way of life is one, but disobedience and self-will may assume a thousand forms. It was worthy of the Divine wisdom to provide a remedy, so far as was possible with the unfallen creature, for this deceptive contrast between the narrowness of the good and the width and largeness of the evil. The twofold nature of man supplied the means for this Divine provision. The body of man was a kind of reflection and image of all the powers of his spirit, and the outward world a mirror for all the unexplored truths of the moral universe. The Almighty Creator condescended, then, to construct a faithful type of man's inevitable probation, and to place it openly before his eyes. The tree of life was a type of the immortal life and unfading joy to be found by communion

with his bountiful Creator, and submission to his wise
and holy command of reverence and love. The tree of
knowledge of good and evil denoted the tempting range
of intellectual enterprise, by which he might seek to pry
out and fathom all the unexplored mysteries of the moral
universe. The rich variety of goodly trees in the garden,
all accompanying the tree of life, proclaimed loudly that
goodness was no narrow and contracted thing, but that
obedience was linked with a large and inexhaustible enjoyment of the Divine bounty. The solitary tree of knowledge, seductive by its name, but standing alone amidst
the large variety of freely imparted blessings, taught that
the way of death, though wide in its seductiveness to the
finite intellect of the creature, was one in principle in the
sight of Omniscience; and its avoidance a small, insig-
nificant sacrifice, amidst such treasures of actual and possible enjoyment. Finally, the solemn warning of the
consequences which would follow the indulgence of this
vain, intellectual thirst for knowledge hurtful to the
creature, completed the economy of Divine benevolence.
The way of life, though narrow in its entrance, was represented in its blessed effects by all the countless flowers
and fruits of Paradise, with the ambrosial tree of life as
the centre and crown of the lovely vision; while the downward path of temptation, contracted within its narrowest
limits, and represented by one forbidden tree alone, was
joined with a warning of its results, so simply and sternly
solemn, that it might have been expected to deter any
sinless creature from ever daring to set his foot within
that dark valley of the shadow of death.

This view of the nature and meaning of the Divine
prohibition rests on no doubtful and fanciful theory. It
results directly from two simple premises, combined to-

gether; the essential laws of moral probation, which a
little calm reflection must reveal, and that typical and
symbolical character of the visible creation, and especially of Eden and Paradise, which is clearly taught us
in the word of God. Once let us recognise this double
truth, and the consequence appears unavoidable. The
tree of knowledge of good and evil was no arbitrary
source of temptation, planted by a sovereign caprice
within the reach of man. It was really a type and pic-
tured image, into which the Divine love had contracted
the possibilities of evil, so as to strip them of their delusive width and vastness, and by a faithful warning to
announce the fatal gulf to which they would lead. And
thus the justice of the Creator is not more signally displayed in the whole arrangement, than the riches of His
wisdom, fulfilling the laws of a pure and deep benevolence. To the eye which has attained any clearness of
spiritual vision, it is a signal proof that the Almighty
has no pleasure in the death of a sinner, but uses every
motive of experience, hope, and fear, to allure his sinless
creatures onward in the happy pathway of holiness, and
to deter them from the tempting, but gloomy and downward road, of sin and misery.

This same view of the typical significance of the Tree
of Knowledge alone reconciles all the allusions to it in the
sacred history. The two rival constructions, which regard
it as a tree of prudence, or a tree connected with the ex-
perimental knowledge of evil, each expresses only half the
truth. The gift implied is the intellectual knowledge of
good and evil, in the full meaning of the terms. God
alone is essentially good, and every creature, by contrast,
in one way or other, in act or capability, in limitation or
defectibility, is essentially evil. (Matt. xix. 17.) Yet the

creature, as God's workmanship, so long as it abides in communion with the Supreme Good, may partake of His goodness, and remain unconscious of its own inseparable shame of mutability, and liability to guilt and ruin. The same knowledge, which to the Infinitely Holy One is the self-consciousness of infinite and exclusive perfection, to the creature is the fatal consciousness of either actual or possible evil, too deep to be fathomed by the thought of man. The All-wise and All-gracious God does not seek, then, to expose the souls He has made to this terrible discovery. He is content to receive from them that narrower and more partial recognition of his creative bounty and goodness, which alone, in their unfallen and sinless state, they are able to render before his throne. He even employs all possible persuasives of heavenly wisdom, to deter them from the fatal luxury of a wider gaze into the vast gulf of all possible things, there to discover the dark shadow of their own possible shame, guilt, and hopeless ruin. But when, in spite of all his gracious prohibitions, they will interpret the commands of his infinite love into the restrictions of a selfish envy, and rush blindly on their own destruction, He begins to unfold the deeper abysses of his own eternal goodness; in order to recover the lost and guilty rebels, so far as they are still recoverable, to holiness and happiness, deeper, fuller, and more enduring, than that which they had recklessly cast away, through the pride that refused to obey the counsels of Infinite Wisdom.

On this view of the tree of knowledge, its relation to the subject from which it derives its name, the knowledge of good and evil, is exactly the same with the relation of the body to the soul of man. It was the exponent selected, by the good pleasure of the Creator, to reveal and embody

a higher truth, which thereby was linked with it inseparably.
All the allusions to it agree fully with this explanation.
When the Tempter solicits the woman, it is with a half
truth, that veiled a practical falsehood. It was true that
their eyes would be opened by tasting the forbidden
tree. It was true that it was pleasant to the eyes, and
a tree to be desired to make one wise. It was true that,
in this one particular, it would render man like God, by
partaking of a knowledge which the Creator seemed to
reserve for his own peculiar prerogative. But the falsehood lay here, in concealing that this knowledge had been
reserved, because it was too awful and solemn for the creature to bear without ruin. The depth of possible evil it
revealed was too fearful for the finite mind to gaze upon,
without being dazzled and overcome. The intellect would
have dragged down the will along with it; since it would
be impossible to look down from a narrow ledge without a
battlement upon a dark and infinite abyss, without being
precipitated headlong by the terrible vision. And it lay
further in the blasphemous suggestion, that God denied
the gift out of envy, and that the threatening, being an
arbitrary act of power, was too severe and unjust ever to
be fulfilled.

The result throws further light on the moral significance of the name. "Their eyes were opened, and they
knew that they were naked." Their nakedness was a fact,
before they tasted of the tree, but until then they did not
know it. They had no consciousness of defect, no sense of
shame, no perception that they stood in need of clothing.
The truth denoted by their nakedness cannot then be
moral evil, since they were naked while still unfallen. It
signified rather the essential defectibility of the creature,
as a creature, which might be veiled by their ignorance,

while they stood in sinless perfection, but was known to their Maker from the first, and as soon as they themselves knew it, was the source of mingled shame and terror. It is not said that the fact of their transgression led to their use of fig-leaves, or to their concealment when they heard the voice of God. Their transgression discovered to them a great truth of their being, which was true before they discovered it. Their terror did not arise, simply and immediately, from the sinful act; but from the knowledge they had attained of the fundamental gulf which separates the defectible creature, liable to every depth of apostasy and rebellious wickedness, from the indefectible and glorious I AM, who alone is incapable of being tempted with evil, and on whom its dark and baleful shadows can have no power. And hence, too, arises the need of a Divine clothing, or that imparted and supernatural grace by which the creature faculties, naked in themselves, are invested with a new life, and put on the beautiful garments of a living and heaven-imparted righteousness.

It results from these remarks, that the sentence of the Judge is no mere irony, as many have held it to be, and have thereby obscured the calm and almost plaintive dignity of the simple announcement—"Behold, the man is become as one of us, to know good and evil." They have already been dealt with as criminals, for their wilful rebellion. They have now to be dealt with as creatures whose intellect has become at once enlarged and diseased, by tasting of the tree of knowledge. They would now have learned, by the bitter effects of the forbidden tree, and the plain contrast with the tree of life, to long, if possible, to repair their error, by tasting of the tree which they had neglected before, and which then would have been a pledge of immortality. But the type was now shattered

by their sin; and what before might have conveyed or preserved life, both for the body and spirit, could now exercise
its virtue upon the body alone. The inner and higher
blessing had been sundered, when sin entered into that
Paradise, which had once been a type of heaven. And
now immortality in the flesh would be a curse, and not a
blessing, and would seal down the fallen spirit in its guilt,
like the rebellious angels, without the hope of redemption.
Hence the expulsion was an act of mingled mercy and
justice—of justice with reference to the original standing
of man in Paradise, and of mercy when considered in the
light of his actual fall. It is not now in yielding to the
instinctive desires of his fallen creatures, that the Almighty can manifest the reality and depth of his own
love. It must rather be proved by that severe and wholesome discipline, which teaches them the exceeding bitterness of rebellion against their Maker; and, writing vanity
and vexation of spirit upon all the joys of sense, shuts
them up to the earnest longing for the promised Redeemer
of the lost, and for their own restoration to the Divine
image; when they shall have access once more to the tree
of life, which blooms for ever in the midst of the heavenly
Paradise.

CHAPTER VII.

ON THE PERMISSION OF SATANIC TEMPTATION.

ONE great perplexity, in the History of the Fall, remains to be noticed; and it is so intimately connected with the later course of Providence, as revealed in Scripture, that it calls for separate consideration. Why was the mighty Tempter permitted to ply his arts upon our first parents, to their ruin? And why, since the Fall, has the same mysterious agency of evil been suffered still to work busily from age to age, as if the Most High designed to aggravate to the uttermost the moral calamities of a fallen race?

We are not at liberty here, without evident falsehood, to resort to the supposition of any strict, absolute, and metaphysical impossibility. The Prince of evil, as a creature, must be under the control of the Almighty Creator; and He who will at last make his sword to approach him in judgment, and execute upon him the sentence of doom, must have been able, from the first, to interdict him entirely from the exercise of his murderous arts, either on our first parents, or on the later generations of mankind. We have here to contemplate an exercise of Divine wisdom, not in the recognition of an eternal necessity, anterior to any positive act of the Supreme Will; but in a sovereign choice, where either alternative, in its own nature, was equally possible. There is no natural, necessary, inevitable connexion between Satanic agency and human probation. The malignant Adversary and Tempter might, from the first moment of his fall, have been sealed in the abyss, and prohibited from all active efforts to deceive the nations. How can we account, then, for the solemn fact which Scripture reveals, that he was permitted to enter even in Paradise, and has continued to exercise his powerful seductions through the long course of six thousand years?

Now it must be plain, first of all, that every arbitrary restraint on the activity of free agents, except as a penal visitation for open crime, must so far violate the simplicity and dignity of God's moral government. The creatures were formed to display the Divine glory. And this can only be by the development of their own powers, so that they may be blessed and a mutual blessing in the right improvement of them, and only in the case of their deliberate abuse the Divine justice be revealed in their deserved punishment. There seems no middle course, consistent with a just conception of the Divine wisdom, between the refusal to create, lest the gift of existence should be abused, or the concession of liberty to every moral agent to manifest freely its own character up to the time of actual judgment, in the full assurance that the wisdom of God can overrule all their acts and purposes, whether good or evil, for some final issue worthy of his own greatness. On this ground alone, it is difficult to see how the Infinite Wisdom could have interdicted the Prince of evil from all activity of seduction, unless by executing the sentence upon him at once for his original crime. But surely the Divine forbearance and righteousness will both receive·

a more signal display by the course of government which Scripture reveals, than if judgment had been inflicted at once upon the lost archangel, before his malice had been proved, in all its intensity of guilt, by his persevering conspiracy against the peace, order, and happiness of the whole moral universe.

But does not such a course wear an aspect of cruelty towards Man himself, the object of these spiritual temptations? Here the question will arise—Were these temptations due to Satan alone, or would they have still existed, had the Tempter been sealed in the abyss? The true answer is self-evident. The secret and inevitable spring of temptation was in man himself, and neither in the Creator nor in the great Adversary. "Let no man say, when he is tempted, I am tempted of God, for God cannot be tempted with evil, neither tempteth he any man. But every man is tempted, when he is drawn away of his own lust, and enticed." The form and circumstances of the trial alone were affected by the permitted activity of Satan. Its substance must have been the same, if the Tempter had never appeared on the scene. The knowledge of good and evil, in their height and depth, as they exist in the region of eternal possibility, would have been equally fatal. The liability of the finite intellect to long after this dangerous knowledge, would have been still the same. The only means of prevention, so far as we can discern, which the Divine wisdom could employ, would be those which were actually employed; to link the inevitable danger with a type, which might serve to show its reality, and the utter unreasonableness of transgression, and to reveal, in a simple and earnest warning, the fatal consequences that must ensue. Left to his own reflections alone, it is conceivable that the catastrophe might be longer delayed; but, so far as we can reason at all on the choice of a free agent, we may reckon it morally certain that the fatal moment would come at last. After all the other trees of the garden had been tasted and enjoyed, the thought—why this solitary restriction, and this too of a blessing, like knowledge, far more precious than all those pleasant fruits which merely gratify the palate—would recur again and again with a fresh seductiveness, and would prevail at last over the fading recollection of the Divine command.

Let us suppose, then, to borrow the conception of our great poet, that the vigilance of the angel watchers had been crowned with success, and the Prince of darkness, detected in his first attempt to transgress the bounds of Paradise, had never been suffered to enter again within the sacred territory. The gain, on man's part, it is highly probable, would have only been a short, and possibly a very short delay, of a sin to which a vain desire of forbidden knowledge would have urged him, soon or late, without the impulse of any external suggestion. But the loss, on the other side, would have been immense. The moral guilt of the crime, on his part, would have been deprived of its chief, perhaps its only mitigation. The whole of that righteous displeasure, which was now shared between the three criminals, and fell chiefly on the malicious Tempter, who knew what would be the consequences of his own success, and delighted in his murderous lie, must then have rested exclusively on Man himself. He would have been, morally, a second Satan, the sole author of his own crime.

But when we turn from the sin itself to the means of recovery, the benevolence and wisdom of God's actual providence, in the permission of Satanic agency, are still

B.   H more conspicuous.   All experience proves that it is a hard and almost hopeless problem to recover a soul, once captive under the power of evil, to purity again.   How can the spirit hate itself?   How can it strive against a mere shadow, which has no separate existence, but dogs its footsteps, and claims to form a part of its own inmost being?

Some help towards this difficult work is found in the duality of man's nature.   The spirit may thus learn to strive earnestly against the flesh, and see in its lusts the ceaseless tempters to evil.   But all the varieties of evil are not easily referred to the bodily appetites alone.   It is a mighty help, then, in the task of regarding evil, not as a part of ourselves, but a separate foe, when we can actually refer every temptation to a real, powerful, and malicious Adversary, who is perpetually bent on leading us astray.   The doctrine of Satanic influence thus becomes one main and most effective engine in the work of our moral recovery.   It is very hard to teach souls, degraded and stupefied by sin, to realize the necessary conflict with evil, in its abstract form, and to view it as a power which must be resisted and vanquished, or else prove their ruin.   But the dullest and most ignorant of men may well be stirred up to seriousness and vigilance, when he hears the Apostolic warning, and recognises it for a revealed and certain truth—"Be sober, be vigilant, for your adversary the devil, like a roaring lion, walketh about, seeking whom he may devour."   And thus the permission of this great Tempter to exercise his utmost subtlety of deception on the minds of men, while it may aggravate the wickedness of the wicked into a fouler intensity, is a powerful means which the Divine Wisdom knows well how to employ, for arresting the careless, alarming the secure, humbling the self-confident, and creating a wholesome and most profitable reaction in the minds of sinful men; by which they may learn to see the nature of transgression in its true light, flee from it as a serpent, and seek for refuge from the dangers which assail their weakness in the protecting care and love of the great Shepherd and Bishop of souls.

We need only to read the Scriptures of the New Testament with care, or study the actual history of the Church of Christ, in order to see the reality of this Divine purpose in the suffered continuance of Satanic temptation. What an emphasis of love it gives to all the history of our blessed Lord himself, that "he went about doing good, and healing all that were oppressed of the devil!" What a startling lesson it reads to the whole Church, when we see the Tempter daring to assail the Son of God in the wilderness, filling the heart of one of the twelve Apostles to betray his Master, and then hurrying him into his awful doom; and again, thrusting in falsehood and deceit into the bosom of the Church, as soon as it was founded, and resisting the progress of the truth, wherever its messengers appeared! And when the word of prophecy draws aside the mysterious veil of Providence, we see the overthrow of this great Adversary linked inseparably with every step of progress toward the world's redemption; so that, until he is finally cast into the fiery lake of judgment, the full brightness of redeeming love, and the perfect reign of peace and righteousness, can never dawn upon our troubled world.

Now if the laws of the Divine government required that the Tempter should be permitted to exert his activity and display his malice, with only a moral counteraction, they would equally imply that no absolute and total restriction should be placed on his use of instruments, which

it lay within the range of his capacity to appropriate and
employ.   The serpent, though sinless in itself, was a form
of life, typical, as science itself seems to show, of evil,
under its features of tortuosity, defect, and degradation.
Its power, in all its varieties, to fascinate, to poison, or to
crush its prey, implies a natural instinct, designed by anti-
cipation to image forth the processes and results of moral
evil.   The introduction of such a creature into Paradise
was essential to its typical completeness, but also implied
a Divine foresight of evil that was about to come.   And
when the mighty Tempter, with the subtlety of an archangel's perverted wisdom, seized on an instrument so
adapted to his purpose, a new means would be provided,
through his own act, for exposing his real character, and
the immense degradation which had passed over his original faculties by their wicked abuse and perversion.   The
enmity between the race of mankind and the serpent
tribe, which formed part of the judicial sentence of God,
became a standing prophecy of Satan's final overthrow.
It proclaimed the Divine purpose that, after enjoying for
long ages no better food for his mighty spirit than the
foul garbage of sin and corruption, he should at last be
completely overcome by the promised Seed of the woman,
and his works of darkness be abolished for ever in the
kingdom of God.

CHAPTER VIII.

ON ORIGINAL SIN.

THE doctrine of Original Sin has always been felt to be one of the most difficult and mysterious in the whole range of Christian theology. The explanations of Divines have been almost as various and conflicting as the objections of unbelievers have been unremitting and zealously sustained. How can millions, themselves innocent, be involved in moral guilt by another's transgression? How can it consist with the justice of God to inflict on them the severest penalty, and even denounce them as worthy of eternal misery, for an act of which multitudes among them never so much as heard, and the breach of a covenant to which they were never consenting parties? And even if such an extension of moral guilt beyond the first agent to millions of his posterity were just in itself, how can that constitution of things agree with the Divine benevolence, which led to such fatal results, and involved a whole race in degradation and moral ruin for a single transgression of their parent, long before their own birth? This is the hard problem, which has exercised the deepest thoughts of reflecting and pious minds, and given birth to various hypotheses to remove the immense difficulty. There is no subject more fundamental to the present inquiry, since no aspect of Providence has suggested so many gloomy and unwilling doubts, or wilful and open blasphemies, against the wisdom and goodness of the Almighty. It has appeared to multitudes in Christian lands a dark and spectral vision, which has scared them away from the revelation of the Bible, to discover a Deity of purer and higher benevolence in the seducing bye-paths of human speculation.

The views of this doctrine among Christians themselves have varied not a little from each other. At one extreme we find the creed of Pelagius, that the sin of Adam affects his race purely by way of example, and that each individual is born into the world in a state answering almost entirely to that of Adam before he fell. At the other extremity of the scale may be placed the high Augustinian view, or perhaps rather the offshoot from it by Illyricus, who maintained that original sin was a positive substance, transmitted from Adam to all his children. Apart, however, from this gross conception, which has had very few patrons, the view itself is, that Adam and his posterity constitute simply one moral person; that they all existed in him from the first, sinned when he sinned, and fell when he fell; that his crime was committed by each of them, as well as by him; that their birth in a mortal state, and with a corrupt will, is the equitable punishment of a sin they have previously committed, as well as the source of all their later transgressions; and that in virtue of it every one of them, infants and adults alike, is justly under the sentence of everlasting torment and misery.

This more rigid form of the doctrine, which Augustine applied consistently to prove the eternal damnation of all heathen and unbaptized infants, has found too little response in the conscience either of worldly or pious men, to have passed current without undergoing various modifications. Two or three of these varieties call for a brief notice.

And first, it has been usual, among the Reformed Divines, to conceive the whole transaction between God and our first parents under the light of a formal covenant, to which the name has been given, the covenant of works. The Creator is supposed to have promised to Adam, for himself and his posterity, eternal life in heaven, after a limited period of probation, as the reward of his sinless obedience to the Divine will, including this one positive test of submission in abstaining from the tree of knowledge. On the other hand, the penalty of disobedience was to be the forfeiture of God's favour and image, and of the grace of the Spirit, and immediate exposure to temporal, spiritual, and eternal death, both for himself and all his descendants. Adam accepted the covenant, not only on his own behalf, but for the whole race. He sinned, and incurred the penalty, which was exacted according to the full width of the original covenant.

The doctrine has been further modified by some recent authors. The main stress is still laid on the notion of a special and voluntary covenant; and a wide contrast is set up between Adam's parental and federal character. But the Adamic constitution, like the Gospel, is said to be a covenant of grace, and not of works. It did not refer to a debt of Divine equity, but to gifts of sovereign grace, bestowed conditionally by charter and covenant alone. The promise was continued life in Paradise, so long as he abstained from the forbidden tree, and included also an assurance of Divine help to keep him from falling in any other way. The result of the fall was subjection to temporal death, and the privation of supernatural grace, with a penal withdrawment of the Holy Spirit, so as to lead to actual transgression in every instance, as soon as the moral faculties begin to reveal themselves. Original Sin, on this hypothesis, is a privation of special gifts, to which man had no claim superadded to his first state of creation. These were bestowed under covenant, on one simple condition, upon Adam and the whole race, and were lost for ever when Adam fell.

Others, to lessen the moral difficulty, would lower the meaning of the penalty. Some affirm that the death of the body is the sole result of Adam's sin to his posterity; while others include the death of the soul, in the sense of annihilation. On their view, natural immortality is a direct fruit and privilege of redemption only. The Articles of the Church of England make Original Sin consist simply in the fault or corruption of man's nature, derived from Adam by natural generation. But, in the systems of most Reformed Divines, it includes another element, and the imputation of the primal act of sin is imagined to precede, and account for, this actual participation of a corrupted nature by all mankind.

These varieties, which might easily be multiplied to a great extent, show the obscurity which still rests upon the doctrine in the minds of thoughtful men. St Augustine, whose writings are occupied with it so largely, and have done so much to fashion it into its popular form, remarks himself that "there is here, perhaps, some secret which is reserved to be made known hereafter, by the grace of God, to holy men." And certainly we may hope, if we follow simply the light of Scripture, and use all the helps that sound reason and an upright conscience can supply, to approach nearer to a just view of the Divine economy, and clear away some of those aspersions which have been so widely cast against the wisdom and goodness of the Judge of all the earth.

I. It will be a first step towards removing the seeming antithesis between the doctrine of Original Sin and the voice of natural conscience, if we observe attentively the real proportions of revealed truth, which have been often departed from, very widely, in human and artificial systems of theology. Some Divines appear to have thought that the history of Adam's fall supplies a strictly logical and scientific key to all the records of sin and wickedness in the later history of mankind, so that every particular sin might be referred to it, and explained by it, like the motions of the planets by the law of gravitation. Hence the personal element in all transgression, which at once appeals directly to the conscience, has been thrown, in their systems, completely into the shade, and a kind of mechanical necessity has replaced the real and eternal laws of moral probation. Such a course, instead of arousing the conscience, has thrown it into a deadly slumber, and puts a plea of fatalism into the lips of the careless and profane, which tends directly to defeat the main object of the Christian revelation.

When we turn to the Scriptures themselves, how different are the proportions in which the truth of God is set before us! We seem to have escaped from a stifling and mephitic atmosphere, where the springs of conscience are weighed down by the incubus of a hopeless necessity of evil, to breathe the free mountain air of heaven, and brace our spirits by the most moving, earnest, and loving appeals, addressed immediately to the individual consciences of men. The fact, indeed, which all experience sets before us, of the wide prevalence of moral evil among men, is recognised in every page; and the wide range and fearful depth of ungodliness in the human heart are portrayed in the most solemn and alarming colours. But it is recognised also, throughout, as an ultimate fact, which the word of God affirms, because it is true, and needful to be known, but does not pretend to resolve it into any prior cause that can render it less mysterious. Never once, throughout the Old Testament, or in the histories of the New Testament, are we taught to explain the dark secret by any reference to the Fall of Adam. Once, however, and only once, in the Epistles of the New Testament, this common relation of the whole race to its first parent is declared to be either the occasion, or the cause, of the universal reign of sin and death. But the simple fact that the Holy Spirit has only once presented the truth of our moral being in this aspect, while appeals to the individual conscience are repeated in every page of Scripture, and almost in every sentence, should teach us how widely artificial systems of theology have often departed from the true standard of practical wisdom, in dealing with the hearts and understandings of sinful men ; and what a prejudice they may thus have created against the whole superstructure of revealed religion, when it seemed to be founded on a doctrine of a fatal necessity of moral evil, destructive to all the moral instincts of our spiritual being.

But besides the utter inversion of the Scriptural proportion of truth in too many systems, by which the attention has been diverted from our own sin to the transgression of Adam, and the individual conscience deadened and pacified with a false and fatal excuse, that

God himself, and Adam our forefather, are mainly charge-
able with our misdoings; when we compare the usual
forms of the doctrine with the simple statements of
Scripture, we can hardly escape the conclusion, that
serious liberties have been used, in the way of addition
and invention, to render it more symmetrical and complete, and fill up the imperfect outlines of one or another
artificial theory. These additions must be firmly cleared
away, before we can hope to see the lineaments of
Divine wisdom and goodness in this fundamental law of
God's dealings with the human race.

And, first of all, the assumption of a formal covenant,
in which Adam contracted with God on behalf of all his
posterity, has no foundation whatever in the inspired
narrative. There was doubtless a covenant, in that
simpler sense which the Greek word διαθήκη naturally
bears; or a disposition and arrangement of the Supreme
Lawgiver, with a command proclaiming his will, and a
penalty on disobedience. But no trace at all can be
found of a mutual compact, and still less of any formal
representation of Adam's unborn posterity. The command to increase and multiply, the gift of dominion over
lower creatures, the statement that it was not good for
man to be alone, and the promise of a help meet for him,
were doubtless generic, and not simply personal, and
would apply prospectively to all Adam's children. But
this cannot prove the existence of any formal and federal
covenant. We should else be driven to the strange inference, that the serpent was a federal and covenant head
to the whole serpent tribe which shared in its sentence,
and Eve a distinct federal head to her own sex, to whom
her own sentence applies in all later generations. Why,
then, resort to a supposition in the case of Adam alone,

of which the Scripture says not a word, and which leads to absurd consequences, when applied to the other parties in the same history?

It has been assumed, indeed, that the transfer of Adam from the spot where he was formed of the dust, to the earthly Paradise, implied a new relation, which was then first assumed, and that a federal character was then superadded to his previous condition, as the parent of the future race. But this also is a gratuitous assumption, without the least evidence in the sacred text. It would be more naturally inferred from the record itself, that if children had been born in Paradise before Adam's fall, the same law would have applied to each member of the race; and that whoever transgressed would alone have been expelled from the holy ground, involving their unborn children in the loss, and have become mortal along with all their own posterity.

A further assumption, even more entirely groundless, is that a limited season of probation was assigned, and the reward promised of translation to heaven, if that period should elapse without transgression. This idea has been justly abandoned by one of the latest writers on the subject of the Fall, as entirely devoid of Scriptural evidence. "From the confidence," he remarks, "with which some men speak where Divine revelation is silent, it is wonderful that they have not assigned the precise duration of the probation allotted to him. The words of the record do not justify such statements. Nothing was expressly promised to Adam. The promise is merely couched in the threatening; and a threatening of death in case of disobedience cannot possibly include more than a virtual assurance of remaining in possession of the life he then enjoyed, if he did not disobey."

Again, to vindicate the wisdom of the federal compact, supposed to have been made with Adam expressly on behalf of his children, an appeal has been made to the powerful motives thus enlisted on the side of obedience. Much eloquence has been sometimes employed, to amplify, on this ground, the aggravated enormity of Adam's guilt, and the wisdom of the original covenant, as increasing the moral probability of man's perseverance. Thus it has been argued by the able writer already quoted : " How unparalleled the force of the motives which were brought to bear upon Adam ! How incredibly superior to those which have been brought to bear upon any other man, except the God-man, Christ Jesus ! The condition of the whole race was practically in his hands. He could bless the world, or destroy the world ; and he chose to destroy it. He put forth his hand, and took the fruit, which denotes the spontaneity of the act, and ate it, and brought death upon himself and the race. Can any sin, even the sin of Judas in betraying his Lord, or the sin of the Jews in crucifying Him, or the sin of the infidel in rejecting the inspired testimony concerning Him, be compared in atrocity with the sin of Adam in eating this apple ? Transgression gathers its guilt from the magnitude of motives to avoid it, and from the amount of ruin and wretchedness into which it plunges. Who, then, can calculate, the guilt Adam contracted, in eating the forbidden fruit ? "

Now far be it from any Christian to extenuate the sin, which experience and revelation have conspired to mark with awful colours. But it is not the less our duty to "judge righteous judgment" in comparing the sin of our first parent with our own. The statement just quoted is excessive and untrue. It would falsify the first principles of Divine equity, since we know that the way of repentance was open to Adam after his fall. But we are told that there is a sin unto death, among Adam's children, for which there is no remedy, and all intercession is forbidden. The sins of parents bring sorrow and misery upon their children still; and each of them has far greater helps for realizing this possible diffusion of the consequences of his transgression, than Adam can be supposed to possess, before the peopling of the earth had begun. His means of knowing the full significance of the threatening were far less than sad experience has given to his posterity; and the exhibition of the Divine goodness in creation is far less complete and glorious than we have received in the gospel of the Son of God. It evacuates all the moral force of the great lesson taught us by the Fall, when we represent the first transgression as some unequalled and unexampled atrocity. The real instruction which it teaches is to be found in the opposite direction. For if a single act of sin, with far inferior light, and scantier experience than we have now attained, has let in upon the world such a sea of miseries, of how much sorer punishment must they be counted worthy, who surpass the guilt of their first parent, sin against clearer and fuller light of truth, and do despite to the Spirit of grace, when he calls them to repentance, and opens to them the way of life once more through the dying agonies of the Son of God?

In reality, the Scriptures themselves yield us no trace of this broad and total contrast between the relation which Adam bore to his own posterity, and that which is sustained by any individual parent with regard to his own progeny. The truth that God visits the sins of the fathers upon their children is stated and enforced many times with reference to others, and only once or twice is applied to him. His standing as the parent of the whole race would alone serve to render him a type of Christ, in a way that would apply to no other person, whose parental influence must be confined to his own descendants. And this parental connexion with a posterity, so as to be a source of a curse or a blessing, is both earlier and more emphatically revealed with regard to others, as Canaan, Abraham, Jacob, and Esau, than with reference to Adam himself. The effects of his sin are doubtless more comprehensive, since they include the whole race; and more visibly conspicuous, since they involve the contrast between sinlessness and a fallen condition. But we ought to pause and require distinct evidence of the fact, before we assume that they rest on some different principle than is involved in every other case of parental responsibility.

With regard to the penalty denounced, there have been opposite deviations from the testimony of Scripture. He must have read its statement with a superficial eye, who can think that the first death, the sentence involved in the original warning, has no reference to the spirit of man, and relates solely to the dissolution of the body. It is clearly an evil influence, described as the rival and adversary of Divine love, to whose secret and constant activity Man thenceforward became a prey. But it departs equally from the tenor of Scripture to confound this result of the fall with the final doom of the wicked, and thus to identify the first with the second death. On the contrary, they form such a total contrast, that the first death is said to be destroyed, at the very moment when the doom of the second death is pronounced upon the guilty at the final judgment.

The aim of the previous remarks is to remove spurious additions, by which the sacred narrative has been overlaid, and the doctrine itself proportionally obscured. Every arbitrary element introduced, to explain the nature of the Divine constitution in Paradise, increases immensely the difficulty of a real vindication of the goodness and wisdom of the Almighty. For if Adam was allowed to stipulate for unborn millions besides himself, in the confidence of a strength which was perfect weakness, and they were all held down strictly to the fatal consequences of his error— if the prohibition was a purely arbitrary test, intended merely to display the Divine sovereignty—if the help of the Spirit, bestowed for every other end, was arbitrarily withheld on this one point only, to give them the opportunity of committing a moral suicide—if the Tempter was allowed to enter, merely to increase the severity of the probation—and if, on Adam's fall, his personal guilt, by an arbitrary act of sovereign power, was charged upon the millions of his posterity, who did not yet exist, and had never sinned, but were created afterwards by separate acts of Omnipotence,—then it must be owned almost or altogether impossible to vindicate the goodness of the Lord in the fundamental laws of his providence towards mankind. But if the true lessons are widely different, and the most solemn features of the history grow out of the eternal laws of moral being, while the elements that were open to the exercise of a sovereign good pleasure were all combined with deepest wisdom, so as to be most favourable to man's recovery out of a ruin that resulted from his foreseen but forbidden iniquity, then we may still adore, with grateful reverence, the grace which mingles with just severity in these counsels of the Most High.

II. Let us now approach more immediately to this great problem of the Divine government. The chief inquiries to be answered are these. What was the real

nature of man's probation before the fall? What was the
nature and purpose of the threatening, and the evil which
ensued to Adam himself, on his transgression? What is
the principle by which the consequences extended and
overflowed to his posterity? How far do these results extend, or what are the distinct effects on the race of Adam's
first sin, and of their own individual ungodliness and transgression? Finally, what reason can be assigned, consistent
equally with the benevolence as with the justice of God,
why a constitution of human nature should have been
appointed at the first, which was foreseen to involve this
tremendous fall and wide-reaching ruin?

A view has been sometimes taken of Adam's probation, which obscures greatly, I think, its real character,
and approaches perilously near to the doctrine, that God
is the author of sin. His uprightness, or the image of
God ascribed to him, is represented as the result of a
supernatural presence and work of the Holy Spirit, by
which he was kept from the possibility of sinning, except
with reference to the one prohibition of the forbidden tree.
He might equally, by the like influence, have been upheld
on that point also, but this help was purposely forborne,
and therefore he fell. His fall was punished by an instant
withdrawal of that supernatural grace of the Spirit he
before enjoyed, and this privation constitutes original sin,
or the universal depravity of mankind. It was a chartered boon while it lasted, and was equitably withdrawn
when the condition of the covenant was broken.

There is one simple scriptural disproof of this hypothesis, besides the evident fact that it is a virtual impeachment of the Divine goodness, and represents God
to have withheld a gift arbitrarily, which it was both easy
and natural to bestow, and to put a solitary restraint on

the inward action of his Spirit, with the express design that Adam might thereby plunge himself and his race into a gulf of misery. The holiness which Adam possessed, so far as it is revealed, is all included and compressed in that one expression, the image of God. But this image was the very gift of creation itself, and not a supernatural endowment bestowed on him after his creation. He was an upright, sinless, moral free-agent, and, so far as the record teaches us, neither less nor more. In those high natural powers of choice, reason, and will, free hitherto from any deflection from the will of the Maker, consisted his original uprightness. He was not created unholy, and holiness bestowed by a separate act, under conditions, as a chartered benefit. His being itself, the moment it was given, was pure and holy. It was a breath of life from God, the effect of the creating power of the Holy Spirit; but when once bestowed, it was pure and holy in itself, and needed no second creation to render it acceptable in the eyes of the Creator. It is said of man, as of the other creatures, when creation itself was finished, that God looked upon him, and he was very good. This reference of Adam's uprightness to a further indwelling and subjective work of the Holy Spirit, distinct from the creative act itself, evacuates the meaning of creation, confounds it with the special processes of redemption, the spotless virginity of the creature spirit with its recovery and bridal glory, and has no trace of evidence in its favour in the word of God.

The influence of the Holy Spirit upon Adam, in the creation state, cannot then be reasonably distinguished from that of the other Persons of the Godhead. That mystery of the Divine nature was still unopened, beyond the personal revelation of the Word, by whom the woman was brought to the man, and who must, probably, have appeared in human or angelic form. There was the objective exhibition of the Divine wisdom, power, and free bounty, to a creature fully qualified to apprehend them by the fundamental law of his creation. No further mode of action on his new-born spirit is revealed. And the more deeply we reflect on the subject, the stronger ground we shall find for the conviction that it was even impossible, without reversing and annulling the faculties of the creature in the moment they were given, or requiring its own consent to their entire suspension, and to a self-imposed passiveness of being, before any reason for this voluntary suicide could be presented to the sinless understanding. The gratuitous hypothesis of a subjective hyper-creation activity of the Holy Spirit, within the mind of the sinless creature, confuses our view of Divine Providence at its fountain-head, and involves unavoidably the result of such an arbitrary withholding of help when most needed, as throws a dark cloud over the perfect love of God, and makes Him the virtual and direct accomplice in Adam's transgression. If a physician were to confine a patient, known to be disposed to commit suicide, in a chamber from which all knives and means of destruction were carefully removed, and were to guard every avenue except a single door, that opened on a precipice and was purposely left wide open, would not the universal conscience pronounce that he was really a party to the fatal crime, although the victim would dash himself to pieces by his own folly?

The supposed provision, then, of a subjective work of the Spirit, by which Adam was kept infallibly from sinning on any other point, has no direct evidence in its favour; and, while it is thought to illustrate the graciousness of the dispensation, really brings a dark, impenetrable

cloud over the attribute of Divine benevolence. In this
case God may have done all that mere justice could demand, and even more; but He would have done much
less than human benevolence, even though imperfect,
would prompt a good man to do.

But the question may now arise—Were there other
conditions, besides abstaining from the tree of knowledge,
a failure in which would have involved the sentence of
death ? Why might not Adam have sinned in any other
way ? And, in this case, what would have been the result
to himself or his posterity?

The true answer seems to be, that inordinate thirst for
forbidden knowledge, in preference to obedience to the
Divine will, is the only way in which a sinless creature
can be conceived liable to fall. So far as God was evidently the bestower of blessings, there was nothing even
for the fallen heart to rebel against, and still less could
there be any temptation to want of love in a sinless creature. Its danger arose from the limitation of its faculties,
and from no actual infection of sin. It must have been
where the desire after something still unknown was met
by a Divine restriction, that the creature would be tempted
to grasp at a seeming good, and to disbelieve the wisdom
and kindness of the prohibition. The tree of knowledge
was planted, virtually, at the first entrance of that Ache-
ronian pathway which led down to the chambers of death.
A deliberate preference of knowledge still unattained,
rather than obedience to God's restraining will, must have
been the real essence of all possible temptation; and when
the type was constructed, in which this moral conflict was
embodied, both in the alluring title of the tree, which was
not concealed from Adam, and in the stern warning of
death, the entrance of sin into the heart of man could not,

perhaps, have occurred in any other way. The two rival
principles, one actually in possession, and the other striving
to allure it, were here brought fairly into conflict, face to
face ; so that the standing of Adam in sinless purity, or
his lapse into rebellion, depended really on this one test
of obedience alone. Other duties, though real, were spontaneous, and free from temptation; but here the mutability and finite knowledge of the creature rendered
probation and danger inevitable.

III. Our next inquiry must be into the nature of the
threatening, and the sentence which it implied. What
is that death to which Adam himself became exposed ?
Was it the dissolution of the body, or did it include the
soul's annihilation, or its moral corruption, or extend still
further to the infliction of eternal and fiery judgment ?
Was it the decree of a sovereign, or the warning of a wise
counsellor, concerning the natural and certain result of
disobedience ?

Now if, laying aside all preconceptions, we read the
narrative in the light of this last supposition, every part
is consistent with itself, and illustrates the goodness and
forbearing love of God. Free liberty was given to enjoy
all the trees of the garden, and eat of their pleasant fruits.
But the warning was given, that there was one tree, to
taste of which would prove fatal, and be followed by death.
While man believed the command to be one of wisdom
and love seeking his real good, he was in safety : as soon
as he suspected it was an arbitrary restriction, capriciously
invented to keep him back from a fuller blessing, the
Tempter had done half his work of delusion, and his fall
was near. Yet this false notion, the fatal result of the
fall itself, cleaves still to nearly every popular explanation
of the narrative, and reads a threatening of arbitrary

power, where there was really the predictive warning of faithful and holy love.

It is true that this idea must be carefully guarded, that it may not lead to danger on the other side. God is not, and cannot be, simply the Friend of his creature; He must also be a Sovereign. When once the command was given, man was bound to obey. His transgression was guilt as well as folly; and the righteous King must have viewed it with infinite and just displeasure. But the moral contrast lies here, whether we conceive the primary character of the message to be the faithful love which warns of a real danger; and only its secondary feature, the sovereign authority which has a right to command, and sees guilt as well as folly in the transgression; or whether it is an act of naked sovereignty, which imposes restrictions merely to show its own dominion, and creates by its own act the danger which it foretells.

On the view of the tree of knowledge, which has been unfolded before, the former is plainly the just view of the Divine warning. We may thus perceive in it the harmonious exercise of all the perfections of the Godhead. The love of the Creator desired and delighted in the continued happiness of his own sinless creature. The wisdom of God foresaw the moral danger inseparable from its limited powers, and devised the means whereby that peril might be made conspicuous, and the most powerful motives combined to dissuade from the downward path. The sovereignty of God, when those means were devised, was exerted to give them a deeper efficacy, and to render the descent impossible, without an act of presumptuous rebellion against a simple and easy command of the Supreme Creator. While man recognised all these characters of the prohibition, it was natural and easy to obey. But when unbelief divorced the power of God, as a Sovereign, from his love and wisdom, the Tempter had won the fortress of man's spirit. He was first persuaded that the command itself was an arbitrary, capricious restriction on his own liberty; and next, that God, although unreasonable enough to give the command, was too kind to enforce so arbitrary and severe a penalty for disobedience.

This view of the history, while it honours the wisdom and goodness of the Divine Lawgiver, is directly established by the order of the sacred narrative. Before the Almighty interferes with any directly penal sentence—nay, even while He has yet to inquire judicially whether the crime has been committed—the tree has realised its predicted character, and the work of death is begun. Their eyes are opened, the fatal gift of forbidden knowledge is gained, and its first effect is to cover them with shame. "They knew that they were naked, and they sewed fig-leaves together, and made themselves aprons." Shame is followed at once by terror. They hear the voice of the Lord God, and hide themselves amidst the trees of the garden. While the inquiry is still pending, the moral desolation is almost complete. Deceit has taken the place of holy peace and confidence, prevarication of truth, and recrimination of mutual love. Death is already busily at work in their hearts. That holier Paradise of the spirit had been as the garden of God before that fatal entrance; and now, while the Judge has not yet opened his lips for the sentence, it is changed already into a desolate wilderness. The predictive part of the warning was accomplished before the decision of the Judge is recorded, and their souls were brought under the awful power of spiritual death.

But the voice was that of a Sovereign, no less than of a Friend, and the rights of sovereignty must be main-

tained, while the truth of the prediction is mournfully
verified.. The outward form of the prohibition, we have
seen, arose from the special appointment of the all-wise
Creator, though the substance was inseparable from created existence. The same relation appears in the fulfilment of the warning. The inner and deeper part was
purely predictive, and fulfilled itself from the very moment
of transgression. But the violated rights of the Sovereign
had further to be maintained, and led to the sentence—
"Cursed is the ground for thy sake. Dust thou art, and
to dust thou shalt return." The essential temptation, in
the desire after dangerous knowledge, was inevitable.
The voice which warned against yielding to it was one of
wisdom and love; and spiritual death was the inevitable,
and not the arbitrary result of the transgression. The
choice of the typical tree of knowledge, as the shroud
for a deep and eternal truth, was due to the sovereignty
of God. So far the voice was a solemn threatening,
and the death of the body was the penalty exacted by
the righteous Judge, as soon as the crime had been
clearly proved.

This view, which results alike from the nature of the
Divine attributes, in their mutual harmony, and from
the order of the inspired narrative, reconciles also conflicting statements, based on a partial induction of scriptural evidence, and avoids the serious errors to which they
lead. Thus many have maintained that the death denounced on Adam was temporal only, since this alone
appears in the sentence of the Judge. This inference
would be perfectly just, if the words were a legal threatening only, since temporal death alone appears in the
legal sentence. But the warning was much more than
a legal threatening, a sanction artificially attached to

a particular crime; and hence the results of the fall are far wider than the dissolution of the body, in turning to its native dust. Others have conceived the doom to be eternal death, or the retributive and final sentence on the ungodly. But this is to contradict scripture, instead of expounding it, since the first death, the result of the fall, and the second death, the result of Christ's judgment, are contrasted with each other in the plainest manner, and the commencement of one is the final abolition of the other. A third class have seen that spiritual and temporal death, together, are the real effect of the fall. But viewing the whole as a purely legal act, they have been embarrassed by a great difficulty—for how can the holy God inflict depravity as a punishment? They have, therefore, substituted a penal desertion of the Spirit for spiritual death itself. But this merely strives to conceal one error by introducing two others; for the creation state of man did not imply a personal indwelling of the Spirit, which is a gift exclusively of redemption. No mention of such a presence, or of its withdrawment, occurs in the whole narrative; it is a gratuitous addition to the Word of God. On the other hand, death is really denounced. So that, on this view, the real consequence is not named, and that is named which God could not inflict without a fearful impeachment of his own perfection. But the whole of these perplexities disappear as soon as we return to the view suggested by the narrative, that simple prediction and warning was the essence of the prohibition, and that the death of the body was a further penal sanction, added to the main sentence, to vindicate the authority of the Lawgiver, whose faithful counsel and plain command had been together cast away.

But when we take the principle already established as a key, it will unlock the words of all the various statements of Scripture respecting the nature and results of Adam's transgression. The death of the spirit is its separation from God, the Fountain of all true life, as the death of the body consists in the loosing of that bond which joins it to the soul. In this deep and awful sense, death is truly the wages of sin. It follows it by no arbitrary act of Divine sovereignty, but by the necessary and eternal laws of moral being. Sin, when it is finished, bringeth forth death. There needs no direct and positive act of Divine interference. Let the Lawgiver forbear to judge, and sin betrays the soul into the hands of God's enemy, the last enemy that shall be destroyed,—a myssterious and awful power, that can sink it deeper and deeper in remorse, destruction, and utter misery ; and no one but the Prince of life has power to lead captivity captive, and rescue the victims of this fatal destroyer, restoring them to holiness and peace again.

CHAPTER IX.

ON ORIGINAL SIN.

THE chief difficulty in the doctrine of Original Sin has still to be considered. Supposing that the Divine economy was just, wise, and gracious, in reference to Adam himself, by what principle are his posterity involved in the fatal consequences of his sin? How far are they, or can justly be, viewed as responsible for the act of their first parent? What reason can be assigned for a constitution, which seems at first sight either positively unjust, or at least harsh, unwise, and severe, and opposed to all the natural lessons of true benevolence?

I. And, first, does the extension of the effects of the fall depend on some arbitrary relation, some special charter or covenant between God himself, and Adam, as a legal representative, consenting to act for others, or does it depend simply on the parental character alone?

The former view has been very widely received. Some recent writers have made this supposed distinction between parentage and federal headship bear the whole weight of the argument, by which they would justify the Divine government. But when we turn to Scripture itself, the hypothesis resembles the Cartesian vortices, and is not only unsupported by direct evidence, but inconsistent with the constant tenor of the inspired declarations. The only key, in the early history, to the extension of the results of the fall is given in the simple words—"And Adam begat a son in his own image, after his likeness." The rescue of Noah, in the deluge, without any special compact beforehand, involved the gift of life to his posterity alone, while all the possible descendants of the rest of mankind were like an untimely birth. They might otherwise have been born, but never came into being.

The curse on Canaan, and the blessing on Shem, without any special compact, passed on to their descendants. The promise to Abraham had the same tenor—"I will be a God unto thee, and to thy seed after thee." When the corruption of fallen man is described in general terms, so far as resulting from Adam's sin, it is referred to the course of natural generation. "Who can bring a clean thing out of an unclean? Not one." "Behold I was shapen in iniquity, and in sin did my mother conceive me." "That which is born of the flesh is flesh." In these and many other passages, the communication of guilt and corruption, so far as they are actually communicated, is ascribed directly to the parental relationship, to the natural course of human generation, and to that alone.

The words of the Apostle in Rom. v. lend no countenance to any other view. He states the fact, that in consequence of Adam's sin death has passed through to all men; but he gives no hint that this wide diffusion of its effects has any other source than the parental relationship alone. Nor does the parallel which he draws require a different view. On the contrary, the fundamental idea, under which the word of God exhibits the diffusion of life from Christ to His people, is expressly that of a spiritual, but real parentage: "When thou shalt make his soul an offering for sin, he shall see his seed, he shall prolong his days." "Behold I and the children whom God hath given me." The communication of natural life in one case, and of spiritual life in the other, is made the evident basis of the whole economy of Providence and grace. The superinduction of an arbitrary element, of which Scripture gives no evidence, merely encumbers the subject with new difficulties. For if the arrangement was not justifiable, wise, and gracious in its own nature, how could any fancied consent of Adam to act on behalf of unborn millions, without any choice of theirs, and when he was ignorant of his own weakness, relieve in the slightest degree the scruples of any thoughtful and intelligent mind?

II. Let us next inquire how far, in the view of Scripture and of reason, the parental relation itself extends? Does it include the body only, or at most the animal life, or embrace really the whole of man's complex being?

This question has caused a great diversity of judgment among metaphysicians and divines. Three main opinions, Leibnitz observes, have prevailed. The first maintains the preexistence of human souls, which are afterwards sent to begin their probation, when the body is prepared. The second, to which Augustine inclined, and which has been usual among Lutheran divines, is the traduction of souls from the parents, along with the body. The third view, more generally received among the Reformed, is that of their creation at the time of each individual birth. He himself propounds a middle theory, that each soul preexists in the parent, as an animal soul merely, and that the faculty of reason is superadded as they are successively born into the world.

The notion of a successive creation has probably been most usual in modern times. Its advocates, indeed, have sometimes denounced the other hypothesis in very strong terms. Thus we read, in a recent treatise on Original Sin, already quoted: "The assertion that one created being actually communicates existence to another, is absurd and impious. A parent is as little (much?) able to create the universe as to impart existence to the soul of the child, or to his body either. God must be regarded as the exclusive agent in the formation of both..... The law of propagation will not account for the character of the race, except on the absurd and profane hypothesis, that the soul is generated together with the body. Even on the absurd notion of the propagation of the soul by generation, its physical properties must originate with God himself!"

It would assuredly be wiser to abstain from such strong expressions with reference to a view held by many orthodox divines, and on a subject confessedly so mysterious. The view thus denounced as absurd, impious, and profane, will be found, I think, the only one consistent with plain and repeated testimonies of Scripture, and also the most agreeable, by far, to the lessons of sound philosophy; while the hypothesis preferred to it is entirely wanting in every kind of evidence, whether of revelation or experience.

And first, we are expressly told that God finished the work of creation, and rested on the seventh day from all his works. Creation then ceased, and Providence began. But if human souls are created successively in multitudes every day, the main work of creation was still future on the first Sabbath. The sacred history is thus contradicted in its main feature. Creation and redemption, on this hypothesis, run on constantly side by side. New-created spirits are formed every moment, to be first steeped in the consequences of a fall, with which they have no native connexion whatever, before they have any part in the blessings of redemption. Such a fact would hold a fore-

most place among revealed truths, if it were really true ;
yet not one hint of it is found from the beginning to the
close of Divine revelation.

Again, there is a perfect symmetry in the actual record
of creation. Vegetables are first formed, the tree yielding
fruit, whose seed was in itself, after its kind ; or with a
natural power of self-multiplication. Next, the fishes and
fowls are created, with the same property, and receive the
law of their creation : " Be fruitful and multiply, and fill
the waters, and let fowl multiply in the earth." The living things of the earth follow ; and the same law, though
not expressed, is clearly implied in their case also. Lastly,
man is created in the image of God, and receives the same
law of increase, after his own kind, as the lower creatures :
" Be fruitful, and multiply, and replenish the earth, and
subdue it." And when the course of human generations
is actually recorded, its conformity to this original law
is recorded also. " Adam begat a son in his own image,
after his likeness." The gift was not the power of propagating animal souls, or mere idiots in human shape, but
of propagating rational creatures, qualified to replenish
and subdue the earth, and to have dominion over the
lower works of God. The opposite hypothesis seems to
deny the fact of a Divine gift, which is expressly revealed,
and substitutes an endless series of direct, successive crea-
tions, for which no grain of evidence can be found in the
whole compass of the word of God.

Again, in the numerous statements of Scripture relative to the birth of children, it is the whole person, and
not the body merely, which is represented as proceeding
from the human parent. The very form of God's covenant involves this fact: "I will be a God unto thee, and to
thy seed after thee." The seed is equivalent to the whole

human being, and cannot, without evident absurdity, be restricted to the body alone. Nay, the promise of God marks the Divine law of Providence still more clearly, in these words of the prophet: "I will sow the house of Israel, and the house of Judah, with the seed of man, and with the seed of beast." What can teach more plainly, that, as every species of lower animal produces its like, so men, and not bodies, are the direct and proper result of the laws of human propagation?

The New Testament continues and repeats the same view. It ascribes the immediate origin of the whole being of the child to its human parent. This doctrine meets us in its first page: "Abraham begat Isaac, and Isaac begat Jacob"—not their bodies, but the human persons. The Apostle tells the Hebrews that "Levi was yet in the loins of Abraham, when Melchizedec met him." And still further, if the law of generation were strictly confined to the animal nature, and could not rise higher, how should it be applied, as it is plainly in the Gospel, to the Divine nature itself, and express that deep mystery of the Godhead on which the whole scheme of redemption depends? If human generation were of bodies only, what meaning could there be in the analogy of that Divine message: "Thou art my Son, this day have I begotten thee"? The Jews inferred from our Lord's assertion, that God was his own father, that He made himself equal with God. But if rational beings generate bodies, or animal souls only, and the rational spirit has to be supplied by a separate and independent creation, the opposite inference would be more just, and the Sonship of Christ would rather prove his essential inferiority of nature.

The words of our Lord seem to crown and complete

the Scripture evidence of this proper derivation of the whole human being from the human parent: "That which is born of the flesh, is flesh; and that which is born of the spirit, is spirit." A great law is illustrated in two opposite forms of its manifestation, and is made the common basis of the reasoning. That law is, that like produces like. But the same principle infers, that a mere animal life will produce a mere animal, and that a rational life will produce a rational being. No offspring can rise above the level of its own parentage, without a supernatural creation; nor sink below it, without a preternatural degradation. Idiocy may produce idiocy; but human parents, without some special agency of the destroyer, in corrupting God's workmanship, and deranging the primal law of creation, must and do produce a reasonable offspring.

The voice of true philosophy is the same. All nature bears witness to the fact, that generation is the highest and most distinctive function of life, in all its varieties. The bee can build cells, and manufacture honey; but its highest gift is the power to continue a race of living architects. The cherishing of their own young is the centre of all animal instincts, and exhibits them in their highest perfection. In the drama of human life, whether real or fictitious, marriage and its mysterious fruits are always the point of culmination. The word of God carries the same law still higher; and shows us that, however wonderful may be the power of God in simple creation, the noblest mystery of the Divine nature lies above and beyond it, in the mysterious and incomprehensible name of the Only Begotten Son of God. It may be affirmed, with much reason, that the idea of a generation of human bodies only, and a direct and independent creation of

B.   K their souls, runs counter to the universal analogy of all creation, and to the uniform testimony of all Scripture. It is merely a legacy of that frigid, corpuscular, mechanical philosophy, imported into theology, which is yielding to the ceaseless advance of natural science. For truth discovers matter itself to be really a magazine of power; and life, in higher natures, to be a mysterious fountain, which overflows perpetually, and tends to rise to the level of its source, however widely its streams are diffused and multiplied.

But it is urged that a parent is as little able to impart existence to the soul of a child, as to create the universe. The notion, it is thought, is absurd and impious. But how can it be impious to believe what is implied in every page of Scripture, or absurd to accept the natural result of daily experience? The voice of common sense instinctively pronounces, that while our first parents must have been immediately formed by God, all their posterity are mediately created, through powers bestowed on their immediate parents. To affirm that God is the exclusive agent in the birth of every human being, is itself the strange absurdity. The facts are plain, and consistent with the deepest philosophy of existence. Trees can produce trees, and animals can produce animals. Human parents also can generate a human offspring, in virtue of a mysterious power of life, given at first by the Creator; but they cannot create either children, or a particle of matter, by a direct act of mere volition. They have plainly a derived and delegated power, but they cannot overleap the limit of the original delegation.

Now if it be true, as Scripture and experience combine to prove, that the whole being of every child of man is given mediately, through powers originally bestowed on our first parents, and not by an independent work of creation at any later time, it is not surprising that many results of Adam's fall should naturally and inevitably overflow, along with imparted life, to his whole posterity, without any separate, penal act of the Supreme Governor. The universal law of all creation would have to be suspended and reversed to hinder such consequences, instead of a special, arbitrary fiat of power being required to bring them to pass. It remains only to inquire how far these consequences extend, and in what way they consist, first of all, with the perfect equity, and next with the real benevolence of the Creator of mankind.

III. And first, it is plain from Scripture, that one consequence of Adam's transgression and fall is the universal exposure of mankind to temporal death. This is implied on the face of the history, when compared with the original sentence : " Dust thou art, and to dust thou shalt return." " Man that is born of a woman is of few days, and full of trouble. He cometh up, and is cut down as a flower; he fleeth as a shadow, and continueth not." " His breath goeth forth, he returneth to his earth ; in that very day his thoughts perish." "All go unto one place, all are of the dust, and all turn to dust again." And it is clear that the death which reigned from Adam to Moses, of which the Apostle speaks, and on which he founds his argument, must refer eminently to temporal death ; since the appeal is to an evident fact of human history, and not to hidden truths of the spiritual world.

Again, it is equally plain that the second death, or the sentence of final judgment on the ungodly, is always referred exclusively to their own personal guilt, and never once to Adam's transgression. Thus we are told, that "every man shall bear his own burden;" that "the son shall not die for the sin of the father, nor the father for the sin of the child;" that "the righteousness of the righteous shall be upon him, and the wickedness of the wicked upon him;" that "every one shall receive the things done in his body, according to that he hath done, whether it be good or bad;" that "the dead are judged every one according to their works;" that "he who soweth sparingly shall reap sparingly, and he who soweth bountifully shall reap bountifully;" that "he who soweth to the flesh shall of the flesh reap corruption, and he who soweth to the Spirit shall of the Spirit reap life everlasting." This great truth of a strictly personal judgment in the last day, according to the individual character—so that each degree of personal righteousness will have its degree of reward, and each degree of guilt few or many stripes in the judgment—is the woof which runs throughout the whole of Scripture, and intersects and binds together its rich promises of Divine mercy and grace. No allusion to the sin of Adam, either as the sole or even a concurrent cause, is to be found in any Scripture revelation of the final judgment.

But the main difficulty still remains—how far actual or virtual sin, and legal guilt and moral corruption, with their effect of spiritual death, are traced directly to Adam's sin, in the case of all his children. For although the sentence of final judgment be directly ascribed to personal transgression alone, still, if that transgression is the inevitable result of a nature vitiated by the act of another, the moral perplexity is not removed.

To solve this hard question, we must first of all recollect the threefold constitution of man's nature, which is affirmed by Scripture, and recognized by the deepest schools of mental science. Man consists of spirit, soul, and body; or, in the terms of one school of philosophy, he has the faculties of reason, understanding, and sense. He has a spirit, or a reasonable will, endued with the power of choice, or self-reflection, and the apprehension of immutable and eternal truth. He has a soul or animal life, similar in kind, though higher and nobler in degree than those which are shared by lower animals. He has an animated body, the organ and vehicle of the soul in its double intercourse, by sensation and appetite, with the outward world. By his spirit, he has fellowship with the angels, and the prerogative of the Divine image. By his soul and body, he stands at the head of the animal creation, and may be included in the systems of universal zoology.

Before the Fall, the union of his whole being was complete. The body was entirely controlled by the animal life; and this lower, animal life, by the higher, rational intelligence and will, which itself was in abiding harmony with the will of the Creator. The natural desire for the pleasant things of Paradise was only the outward expression of the Maker's will, when He said, "Of every tree in the garden thou mayest freely eat." The inner subordination of human nature was complete. But when temptation prevailed on the one point, where the natural, sinless desire was withheld from act by a Divine prohibition, and the conscious will affected the revolt, the whole frame of man's being was loosened and disjointed. The body, only imperfectly subject to the life within, received the seeds of death. The animal life, no longer in perfect union with the reasonable will, became a source of ungoverned and tumultuous appetites, that craved their own indulgence for their own sakes, apart from the voice of conscience, or the will of God. And the will itself, conscious of its own wilful transgression, became subject to shame and fear, that would tend to lead it into a gulf of utter despair, without some interposition of grace; since the conscience and the reason could themselves devise no way of deliverance from the curse of the violated law of God. The mere contemplation of God in his holiness would now become alarming and terrible, and repel the spirit further and further from the only Source of true life and light into outer darkness.

When we turn from Adam to his posterity, the propagation of this evil state, with respect to the soul and the body, seems to be the clear voice of Scripture, reason, and experience. "That which is born of flesh is flesh," and "the minding ($\phi\rho\acute{o}\nu\eta\mu a$) of the flesh is enmity against God, for it is not subject to the law of God, neither indeed can be." The animal nature, once loosed from its original standing of perfect union with the pure and reasonable will, is propagated in its actual state, as a natural or animal man, with no instinctive submission to any human or Divine rule of right or wrong. This infection of nature remains, even in the regenerate. The sinful habits, or holy disposition and practice, of the immediate parents, may increase or lessen its intensity in their children; but the fact itself is a law of universal experience, confirmed by the whole tenor of the word of God.

But what shall we say with regard to the spirit itself, the seat of conscience, the highest and noblest part of human nature? Is a sinful will directly propagated, in the same manner as a sinful nature in the animal being? If we confine the effect of the Fall to the lower and separable elements of our nature, do we not come short of the statements of Scripture, the lessons of sound theology, and the facts of experience? If we say that the will is propagated from the human parents, and under the actual dominion of evil, do we not make God virtually the Author of sin by such a constitution, and so undermine the very foundations of conscience and of all just ideas of moral government?

There are two or three facts, either revealed in Scripture, or deducible from close reflection on the nature of conscience, which will perhaps go far to remove this difficulty, and help us to approach, at least, to a just view of this mysterious arrangement, that seems at first hard to reconcile with the wisdom and goodness of the Almighty.

And first, it is clear that the spiritual effects of the Fall on Adam and Eve, which alone are recorded, were the direct fruit of their own consciousness of a personal transgression. They knew that they were naked, and were ashamed. They heard the voice of God, and hid themselves in fear from his presence. They knew themselves guilty of a wilful act, and sought to throw the blame upon others, Adam on Eve, and Eve on the Serpent. In the whole of this mental process, the consciousness of their wilful act was an inseparable element. This working of death in the inner sanctuary of the spirit, so far as we can gather from this first record of Scripture, could not be propagated, unless the individual personality could be propagated, which is evidently impossible. A like consciousness of guilt in the spirit, from a similar cause, may arise afterward in Adam's children; but the consciousness of that personal sin, which wrought fear and shame in our first parents, cannot be transferred. To the sin of Adam, in this one view of it, the words of the Holy Spirit must apply, that every man shall bear his own burden. This could not be, if the personal act of Adam, of which he alone was the conscious cause, was reckoned to each of his children in the list of their own acts of personal transgression.

Again, it is a revealed truth that children, before their birth, and some time after, have no such knowledge of good and evil, as originates a moral responsibility. Thus it was said to the Jews in the wilderness: "Your little ones, which ye said should be a prey, and your children, which in that day had no knowledge between good and evil, they shall go in thither." Of the promised child Emmanuel, it is written, "Butter and honey shall he eat, that he may know to refuse the evil and to choose the good. For before the child shall know to refuse the evil, and to choose the good, the land thou abhorrest shall be forsaken of both her kings." The Apostle remarks of Jacob and Esau, while unborn, as a self-evident fact, that they had done nothing either good or evil. And the words in the history of Jonah respecting the children of Nineveh, who knew not their right hand from their left, may be reasonably transferred to the higher subject, the faculty to discern between moral good and moral evil. To crown these testimonies, the Apostle James lays down a principle, which may clearly be viewed as a universal axiom of morals, excluding sin on the one side, and defining it on the other: "To him that knoweth to do good, and doeth it not, to him it is sin."

Experience and philosophy illustrate and confirm these truths. There is a law observed in the natural propagation of life, by which its development ascends through the lower to the higher functions. The power of assimilation, or vegetable life, is first developed. The embryo is then quickened, and acquires the power of spontaneous motion. The development of a self-conscious, reflective intelligence, must be a still later stage. All the later faculties are virtually included in the first production of new life, in all its varieties, from the lowest insect up to man himself; but there is an order in their actual exercise and possession. Moral responsibility, and the proper consciousness of guilt, can only begin with the possession and exercise of a personal will, capable of knowing good and evil, and at liberty consciously to choose between them.

Let us now conceive a case which has never occurred, but which throws light on the moral elements of the problem. We may imagine the new-born will, as soon as it awakes to a consciousness of good and evil, to choose the good continually by its own strength, and reject the evil in spite of the strong seductions of that animal nature which is born along with it, and has become disjointed from the spirit by the effects of Adam's fall. Such a being, sinless in will, could not be treated as a guilty, wilful rebel, without contradicting the fundamental laws of Divine equity. It could not, however, dwell in the presence of God, and the enjoyment of His perfect favour, without a like contradiction of His spotless holiness. It must remain, for a season, under probation. Persevering inwardly in its uprightness, it could not cease from that probation, till the animal life had been destroyed, in virtue of its corruption, and the spirit had endured, without murmuring or rebellion, or deviation from entire obedience, the full weight of the Divine aversion to a nature that has broken loose from its original law, and rebelled, to the extent of its own faculty, against the will of God. But if this severe probation were endured without failure, the sinless will must be doubly acceptable to the God of holiness, beyond the sinless angels, from the trial which it has endured, and the severer test of its unswerving allegiance to the Divine will. This fearful gulf would have to be traversed, and then a Paradise of joy and peace would greet the spirit on the other bank of the dark river of death. But a failure in this necessary trial would let in sin to the sanctuary of the spirit; and its recovery, when once fallen, by its own efforts, would be utterly impossible.

Such, however, is not the character of the human will, when it first awakes to individual consciousness, and the sense of personal responsibility. It cannot, it is clear, have that disposition to evil which results from habitual transgression, nor that remorse which arises from the consciousness of personal criminality. In these respects there is an innocency of childhood, to which our Lord seems to refer in those words: "Of such is the kingdom of heaven." On the other hand, it has the mutability of all free agents, the nescience and weakness of childhood, and is surrounded by the urgencies of a fleshly nature, which has broken loose from its entire subjection to the spirit of man and the laws of God. If Adam fell, in sinless perfection and the strength of mature reason, when there was no internal discord to mar and disturb the harmony of his own being—then a will, so circumstanced as has just been described, will be sure to fall. The moral declension from the holy and perfect rule of the Divine law, which appeared in Adam as a grievous, inexcusable abuse of freedom, will here approach to the features of a fatal necessity. Yet since a right choice must still have have been possible, or man would not be a moral agent at all, and the law of right is binding by its own authority, and can suffer no circumstances to excuse transgression—this moral necessity, which may be allowed to exist, is still removed by a wide gulf from a purely physical fatality, which would destroy the foundations of all moral government.

But the hypothesis, just considered, does not express the real facts of human probation. It exhibits a part of the truth, but not the whole. Before Adam became a parent, and even before his expulsion from Paradise, the economy of redemption began. The revelation of God's name was no longer confined to his goodness in creation, the holiness of his law, and his anger against rebellion; it included a promise of grace to the fallen. Before any curse was pronounced, inclusively, on mankind, as the children of Adam, they had all of them, inclusively, received a significant promise, as the offspring of the woman. The special and emphatic meaning of the phrase, the Seed of the Woman, which time has disclosed, cannot set aside its more immediate and wider reference to the posterity of Adam, as all woman-born, in contrast to the serpent race. This meaning of the promise is formally sealed, in the name, which the woman receives from her husband, before the guilty pair themselves are excluded from Paradise. And hence every child of Adam, from its birth, would enter on its probation, not only with the adverse effects of the fall around it, which would tend to drag down its will into a course of fatal disobedience and ungodliness, but under the canopy of a Divine promise, addressed to it as also a child of Eve, and with a way of life opened before it, which would lead upward to peace and happiness again.

These views of the consequences of the Fall, and of

the nature of original sin, may be thus briefly summed.
All mankind were created, seminally, in Adam, by virtue
of that mysterious and wonderful power which the Creator imparted from the beginning, when He said—"Be
fruitful, and multiply, and replenish the earth." The
work of creation then ceased; and a later, successive,
independent creation of human souls adds to the word
of God what it has nowhere revealed, and sets aside its
express statement with regard to the nature of the gift
originally bestowed. We read, accordingly, in Gen. vi.,
that the Adam was multiplied upon earth. Hence all
mankind are naturally, and necessarily, by the law of
their creation, involved in the results of his fall. So far
as these relate to the lower, animal life, and the body,
they follow simply and absolutely, by the law of propagation. "That which is born of the flesh, is flesh,"
and naturally resists the restraints of the Divine law, and
becomes the source of perpetual temptation to the reasonable will. The will, or highest part of man's nature, is
also derived from the human parent, but in a latent or
nascent form, and only acquires a consciousness of distinct
personality, and along with it, moral responsibility, after
the natural birth. Left to its own mutability and weakness, and temptations of the flesh alone, it would fall,
even more certainly than Adam fell. The whole being
of man—spirit, soul, and body—would then become entirely depraved and ruined. Even apart from its own
fickleness or perverseness, the difficulties opposed by the
fall to its full recovery, in a persevering resistance to all
evil, far surpass the probable measure of any created
virtue. But each child of man has not been left to these
results of the fall, without any countervailing influence.
By virtue of his birth into the world he becomes also

one of the seed of the woman, and thereby is brought within the scope of a gracious economy of redeeming love. The conflict of good and evil, in which his first parent was overcome, is renewed in other forms, and mightier influences are arranged on each side than before. The great Deceiver bends all his skill to complete his conquest, and detain his prey in a hopeless captivity of evil; and the world and the flesh are his allies in the work of ruin. But a mighty Redeemer, who is stronger than he, has also begun his work of love, and pours out the stores of his heavenly wisdom in promises, warnings, example, invitations, threatenings, and messages of grace, that He may recover the lost sheep out of the dreary wilderness of sin, and bring them back on his shoulder, rejoicing, to join the family of heaven.

The Fall, then, as it affects the soul and body, in the special sense already defined, is accomplished once for all—a sorrowful certainty, that encompasses every child of man from the hour of his birth. But as a still deeper fact of the spiritual being, it is repeated perpetually, when the new-born conscience wakes up to the sense of its own powers, and the new-born will first departs from that moral rule which asserts its own unalterable claims. But, before the first of Adam's children was born, a Divine remedy had also been provided; and the voice, which announced enduring enmity between the seed of the woman and the seed of the serpent, opened a new world of hope to "man that is born of woman, and full of trouble," by which to reclaim his spirit, upward and heavenward, into the path of recovered peace and holiness.

It is therefore a great departure from the standard of

truth, to excuse our own sins by charging our first parent
with a guilt of unequalled atrocity. His sin indeed was
great and inexcusable, and its consequences most grievous; but the sin is heavier of those who despised and
rejected the law of God, as given by Moses; and heavier
still, of those who trample under foot the Son of God,
by rejecting the Gospel, and do despite unto the Spirit
of grace.

IV. It remains now to consider what light can be
thrown on the reasons for this mysterious constitution of
human nature, proceeding in successive generations from
one common parent, and involved in his fall; and how
far we may read in it a new lesson of the wisdom and
benevolence of the Almighty.

Before the creation of man, the history of angels, and
the rebellion by which multitudes of them had fallen, revealed in a most impressive and solemn light the mutability of all created free agents. No circumstances, we
may well suppose, could be more favourable for continued
stability than theirs. No temptation from without assailed them; no burden of flesh confined and limited
their being. They were created godlike, with as near an
approach to Divine perfection as creaturehood would
allow; and we read of no positive ordinance superadded
to the great universal law of obedience and love. But
their greatness was turned by pride into the occasion of
their ruin. The foremost and brightest, the Son of the
morning, fell; and a large proportion of them became
his partners in daring rebellion against the Almighty
Creator.

There are thus two main reasons which may be conceived to lie against a second angelic creation. Such a
creation, in its very conception, must be finite and

incapable of increase, and thereby fall short of a full reflection of the Divine infinity. And when sin has once entered, as it had now shown its power to enter, there seems to be no way of possible recovery. The simplicity of their spiritual being appears to preclude the separation of the fallen and rebellious will from its own perverseness. Their fall was an entire and hopeless ruin.

It became the wisdom of the Almighty, in his further works of creation, to provide against the fearful dangers, the reality of which, in the case of his intelligent creatures, had now been so sadly and terribly established. A second race of angels would have been exposed to the same dangers with the first, with the added perils of a systematic, powerful array of spiritual temptations, and the fears that might well be awakened by the knowledge of others' fall, and of their own mutability, with no visible contrast to assure them against the ever-threatening danger of plunging into the same gulf of sin and ruin. The furthest and deepest revelation of the Divine character would thus be one of distributive justice only; and His creatures might be tempted to regard Him as a severe Judge, who created them indeed with high and noble powers, but placed them on a dangerous pinnacle of being, and, standing out of the reach of temptation himself, abused his power in the severe punishment of his own offspring, while they were drifted successively away from his holy presence into unsuspected pitfalls of moral degradation by secret and awful influences of inevitable evil, that seemed justly to dispute with the Most High God the dominion of his own universe.

In the creation of man a provision was to be made for these deeper objects of the Divine government, which grew out of the proved existence, and awful intensity and subtlety, of moral evil in spiritual beings. And first of all, a new attribute was bestowed, which rendered the new creature a closer resemblance of the life-imparting power of the Creator; and gave the new race, in its original constitution, a passive infinity, a capacity of boundless and illimitable increase, as the stars of infinite space, and as the sand by the sea-shore innumerable. But a still further object had to be attained. Instead of an arrangement for the stability of the new creature, it was the deeper lesson of wisdom, to provide all, and arrange all, even in the hour of creation, to meet the moral certainty of an approaching fall. Creation and sinless purity is the key-note of angelic being, but redemption is the master-key of the history of mankind.

To secure this great end, there were three main conditions which had to be satisfied in the constitution of the new race of moral agents. These refer to the subjective and objective possibility of redemption from the power of evil, and the choice of circumstances most favourable to the reception of those great truths of the spiritual world, by which alone the great work of recovery could be successfully and powerfully carried on.

To render this redemption of the fallen subjectively possible, the creature must be so formed as to admit of an actual, internal separation from the evil which has gained an inward mastery. And this appears to be one great purpose of the actual constitution of human nature. The fallen will is taught to project its own corruption upon the flesh which has proved its tempter; and hating its own life, under this evil and corrupted form, can set out in the pathway of repentance, and receive the better life of the spirit. It is by the sacrifice of the polluted, animal life, the crucifying of the flesh, with its affections and lusts, that the whole internal process of redemption has always been carried on. That companion of the spirit, against which it so often frets in its pride, and which makes it, by creation, a little lower than the angels, is the means, by its own death, and the willing consent of the spirit that it should die, of its recovery to perfect holiness again. The duality of man's nature, while it places him below angels, renders fallen man internally capable of being redeemed.

But redemption needed also to be objectively possible. There behoved to be some means provided, by which the holiness of God might be fully cleared, in visiting a second race of intelligent creatures, guilty of rebellion against his laws, with the promises of his favour, and the hope of recovered peace. If it was the design of God to unfold towards the new race his deepest attribute of mercy, and to meet them with all the varied appliances and hopes of a new economy of redemption, it was needful that there should be, objectively, with reference to the whole race, a capability of manifesting the spotless perfection of his justice as the Moral Governor of the world. There was not only to be solved the question of individual equity, with regard to each member of the race, but the Thrice Holy was himself to be justified in departing from the rigour of a sentence, like that which rested, without change or hope, upon the angels that fell. No one but the Eternal Word could satisfy this demand of infinite wisdom ; and it was one condition required in the new creation, that the Word might be capable, by an act of incarnation, of linking himself at once with the whole race, and thus reveal in his own person the harmony of justice and infinite love.

B. L

But it was eminently the part of Divine wisdom to devise such a constitution for the new race of creatures, that the great moral truths, on which their recovery would depend, might be clearly and forcibly brought out in relief before each individual, when he first entered on his term of probation. What then are the most important and fundamental of these truths? How did holy angels fall from their first integrity? First of all, through their entire inexperience of the deep curse and practical misery of all moral evil, which left them open to the delusion of conceiving it a vast unexplored region of happy independence and godlike liberty of being. Secondly, the self-dependence of a purely spiritual nature, that, being so highly endowed, forgot the wide gulf which separates the mutable creature from the immutable Creator, and through pride broke loose from the golden chain of obedience which bound them to the throne of God. And thirdly, when they had fallen, not only the simplicity of their nature seems to have rendered their redemption subjectively and objectively impossible, but there was no way by which a deeper attribute than simple justice could reach their rebellious will, and reclaim it into repentance; and the spiritual repulsion of the unholy from the spotless holiness of the Most High seems to have hurried them swiftly into a gulf of utter separation, where no glimpse of light could dawn upon the thick darkness of their inward being.

Now the constitution of man, and the successive birth of each individual into the world under the circumstances which result from Adam's fall, eminently satisfy all these conditions. The creature has been made subject to vanity, not willingly, but for the sake of man; and from the first cry of infancy, when it enters into a fallen world, all is full of sad but profitable lessons of the vexation of spirit, which is the fruit of rebellion against God; and the experience of all mankind, accumulating from age to age, rises in the face of every new child of the dust, to say that it is an evil and a bitter thing to wander from God into the dark by-paths of moral evil.

But the angels fell by pride, no less than by inexperience of the miseries of sin. Their godlike faculties raised them so near the throne, that their leader was tempted to the awful experiment of setting up for the rival and adversary of his Creator. And what means could be so powerful for abating pride, and bringing the creature into its safe and right state of dependence upon the arm of its Creator, as that fearful and wonderful workmanship, the nature of man? He was fashioned out of the dust at first, and since the fall is turning continually to dust again. And this is not the whole lesson of humiliation. By a humbling pathway, over which the instincts of his nature compel him to draw a veil of silence and secrecy, he comes into being, and his will begins its course of self-conscious responsibility amidst all the weakness and dependence of infancy and childhood. How powerfully is his spirit thus allured into its true position of simple, childlike dependence upon the arm of God! Thus we are reminded that God perfects strength out of the mouth of babes and sucklings; and the moral heroes of our race have the lesson taught them, by their own birth, as well as from the lips of Infinite Wisdom, that except they become in spirit as little children they cannot enter into the kingdom of heaven.

The third condition, favourable to moral recovery, is also fully satisfied in the actual constitution of mankind. We cannot escape, from our birth, the voice of those

Divine messages which tell of goodness that still visits
the unthankful and unworthy, and invites them back to
the arms of Divine love. The light may shine more
dimly on lands long sunk in spiritual darkness by their
own rebellion; but it cannot be extinct, while man is born
of woman, and enters on a world where sinners every
day breathe the air of heaven, are warmed with the sun-
shine, and refreshed and nourished by the showers of
rain and the plenteous fruits of the earth. Man, however vicious, cannot in this life sink himself into an outer
darkness, where no beam of Divine love reaches the fallen
spirit, to attract it upward into the region of purity and
peace again. He walks under the blue sky, which de-
clares the glory of its Maker, and bends down over him
on every side, as if to embrace him within the arms of an
infinite and Divine compassion. He moves amidst the
hills and valleys, which the Creator's hand has clothed
with beauty, and which drink their life continually from
the dews of heaven. "The earth is full of the goodness of
the Lord." But goodness, so plentifully displayed towards
conscious sinners, is mercy begun. Even where the noon-
day brightness of the Gospel has not appeared, its dawn-
ing light visits the nations, and looks down upon the soul
from every star in the firmament, while it beams with
a calm and holy light upon spirits that might well be
visited with severe strokes of Divine judgment. The
things which are made not only proclaim the power and
Godhead of the invisible Creator, but are an hourly
witness of his forbearing mercy; while He shows kindness to the undeserving and the guilty, and makes his
sun to shine on the evil and the good, and sends rain
upon the just and the unjust. All things around them,
from the cradle to the grave, are teaching mankind the

threefold lesson : that sin is certain misery—that their
native strength, for regaining the lost image of the Creator, is the helplessness of mere infancy—and that they are
not cast off into a region of hopeless despair, but are still
the prisoners of hope, and shut in on every side with abun-
dant tokens of their Maker's undeserved and persevering
goodness. By a thousand acts of bounty and wisdom the
wandering prodigals are allured to return once more to
the true home of their spirits ; to find, through penitence and prayer, that way of life which still lies open
before them, and to experience that richest of all earthly
blessings, which constitutes the delightful foretaste of
heavenly felicity,—

   " A Father's kindness in a God of love."

CHAPTER X.

ON THE INCARNATION.

THE doctrine of the Incarnation, or in Scripture language, that the Word has been made flesh, and dwelt among us, and that Jesus is the Christ, the Son of God, is the foundation truth of Christianity. It has naturally been encountered by a large variety of difficulties and objections. The bitter controversies to which it gave rise, in the fourth and following centuries, have lent a keen edge to the sarcasms of sceptical writers; and the syllable which parted Arianism from the orthodox creed, and the prepositions used in the subtle disputes of the Fourth General Council, have given repeated occasion for contemptuous declamation on the folly of theological controversies.

We cannot wonder that a doctrine, so mysterious in its own nature, and surrounded by such an atmosphere of spiritual litigation and debate, should awaken many doubts in some thoughtful and serious minds. How can we reconcile an incarnation with the Unity of the Godhead? How can we conceive that two wills, the uncreated and the created, should coalesce into one; or that remaining two, they should constitute only one personal agent? Why should the race of men receive a privilege so peculiar, and so impossible to be repeated for any other race of beings, without introducing conceptions altogether incredible? And if we admit the reality of a condescension so strange and wonderful, how is it that the moral effects are so limited and partial? After such an act of Divine condescension, how is it that the adversary can still hold in bondage the greater part of that race, which has been taken into union with the Godhead itself, the uncreated essence of the Most High?

The objection, so far as it relates to the essential nature of the Divine Being, and the conceivableness of such an act of condescension, does not come within the scope of my present inquiry. My aim is to deal with the difficulty on its moral, rather than its metaphysical side; to show that such a union of the Divine nature with the human, its possibility being assumed, is both good and wise; that the object to be attained is worthy of the Divine wisdom and love; and that sceptical doubts gain their only seeming strength from dwelling upon the past alone, and refusing to recognise the truth of God's revealed promises concerning the width and grandeur of redemption, and the glories of the world to come.

And first, every communication from God to his creatures must involve an infinite condescension. He who is unsearchable cannot have his nature or perfections fully comprehended by a finite understanding. The words of the Apostle, when he contrasts the partial knowledge of this life with a perfect knowledge in the life to come, ought not to be strained beyond their due limit; so as to overlook his own illustration from the knowledge of a child, in contrast to that of the full-grown man. All our experience of Providence on earth, the statements of Scripture as to the lessons learned by angels from the history of the Church, and the promises of the perpetual increase

of Christ's kingdom, conspire to prove that the felicity of
the life to come includes a ceaseless progress in wisdom
and love. The creature, by the necessary limits of its
being, cannot attain absolute infinity. But it may attain
and enjoy the relative infinity of rising nearer and nearer,
for ever, to the full apprehension of the Divine goodness.
The time may come when the least in the kingdom of God
may surpass the present attainments of the foremost Apostle, or the highest archangel. But the disparity may still
remain as great as it is now among the hosts of the redeemed children of God. Every communication made to
a finite capacity must stoop to the level of the recipient.
And hence it would seem that a virtual incarnation is implied in the very idea of a message from God to men.
Unless the Most High were to veil himself from all his intelligent creatures in clouds and thick darkness, which no
eye of man or angel can penetrate, there must be a thousand repeated acts of Divine condescension to the bounds
of angelic or human nature. And these appear to involve
the principle of an incarnation, though they may not alone
avail to establish a fact so wonderful as the real and per-
manent union of the uncreated Word with one of the
reasonable natures He has made.

Now if some condescension of God to his creatures is
virtually implied in the very fact of a revelation, and its
fuller exhibition is suitable to the dignity and harmony of
the Divine government, its most reasonable form must
surely be when the nature assumed is eminently central
to the whole universe of created being. When we compare in this respect the only two races of rational creatures
whose existence is known to us, there is one plain reason
why human nature, rather than that of angels, should
receive this honour. For man occupies a central place

among all the works of God. His spirit links him with
the hosts of angels, and he is only a little lower than they.
But his animal life links him equally with the whole range
of animated being, and his body, in its material substance,
is no less connected by the laws of gravitation and chemical affinity with the planetary spheres, and the whole
inorganic universe. His inferiority to angels, as less simple and purely spiritual in his being, is compensated by
the variety of the bonds which thus unite him with all
creation, from the mote that dances in the sunbeam, or
the insect that sports among the flowers, up to the loftiest
seraph who veils his face in the immediate presence of the
Divine glory.

Now if it were the purpose of God, in taking a created
nature into union with himself, to manifest the goodness
which unites Him perpetually to all his works, then of all
forms of being actually known to us, human nature is the
most suitable to this great design. The Son of God has
hereby united himself with all the forms of created existence, through man, who is closely linked with them all;
and still further, with all degrees of rational intelligence,
from the latent, undeveloped reason of the new-born infant, up to the noblest eminences of celestial and seraphic
wisdom. The work of love, once for all to be accomplished, is thus realized in the most comprehensive form
which it is possible for us to conceive.

There seems to be a further reason for this preference
in the closer intimacy of union thus attainable. Every
angel is a separate creature of God. We may conceive one
fresh individual of this kind to be created, and a union,
like that of the incarnation, to be effected with it by
Divine power in the moment of its birth. But it would
be a union with that one angel alone. The whole race of

mankind, on the contrary, as they proceed from one root
or source, are partakers of one common nature. The Son
of God, in assuming it, became intimately united with every
child of man whose created being is derived from Adam
and Eve. The Mediator of God and Man is the Man
Christ Jesus. The law of creation, in the case of man,
has thus provided, with deep foresight, for what seems a
fundamental necessity in the great work of redemption.

Again, it was fit that this most surpassing proof of
Divine goodness, the real union of the Godhead eternally
with a creature being, should be reserved for the deepest
claim of love, and that hardest work, which demands the
exercise of all the moral perfections of the Almighty.
That work is redemption; or the recovery of moral agents,
endowed with free will, and still retaining the power of
choice, though now in bondage to evil, out of that gulf
into which they have plunged themselves by rebellion and
disobedience. The creation of man, we have seen already,
in contrast to that of angels, has reference throughout to
a coming work of redemption from a foreseen fall and
ruin. And hence there is a deep congruity between the
very constitution of human nature and that central work
of Divine love, whereby the Son of God, assuming our
mortal flesh, came to bear up the pillars of a sinking universe. The work of the six days did not more truly point
forward to the creation of man, the destined lord of all the
lower creatures, than the nature of man himself, with an
eye which could pierce into the secret moral causes of
things, pointed onward to a coming fall, and the sure promise of a recovery, to be wrought by the Word of God,
invested for that end with a new and mysterious title,
the Seed of the Woman. He " is before all things, and
by him all things consist." Man, in the hour of his crea-

tion, was fearfully and wonderfully made; so that his
nature, beyond that of angels, was capable of receiving
the vast and inestimable treasures of Infinite Love.

There is a further reason which may, with reverence,
be assumed to exist for this choice of man's nature to be
adopted into the Divine. For the nature thus assumed,
in its original constitution, admits of a perpetual increase,
by which it may reflect, in the largest measure conceivable,
the absolute and infinite fulness of the Uncreated Being.
This capacity of human nature, now marred and defaced
by the Fall into a thousand shapes of vice and impurity,
is assumed, in the form of hope most current among
Christians, to be never repaired into its original dignity,
but to be extinguished for ever. The thousands of generations, or perpetual generations, of which the Scriptures
speak so often with accents of hope and praise, dwindle
down, in the usual form of Christian hope, into less than
two hundred, which alone can be crowded into the narrow
limit of seven thousand years. But if once we accept
those statements in their natural meaning, and cease to
limit the range of redemption to the Church of the First-
born alone, the firstfruits in the harvest of the new
creation, a further and powerful reason will appear why
human nature should be selected to receive this highest
gift of the Creator's love.

All the earliest promises of the Messiah are accompa-
nied by some express allusion to this prolific virtue,
impressed on man's mysterious being. When the Seed of
the Woman is announced as the world's Redeemer, to
crush the head of the serpent, the promise to Eve instantly follows :—"I will greatly multiply thy conception."
In the covenant with Abraham, the promise of the Seed
who shall possess the gate of his enemies is joined with

another, of increase as the stars of heaven and the sand of the sea shore. And when Isaiah renews the hope in those tones of rapturous praise, " Unto us a Child is born, unto us a Son is given," the promise at once follows, that " of the increase of his government there shall be no end."

An objection, however, has often been conceived to lie against the doctrine of the Incarnation from the discoveries of modern science. The telescope reveals myriads of suns and systems, scattered throughout the depths of infinite space. Can we conceive, it is asked, that all these systems, compared with which our earth is a mere speck, are devoid of rational and intelligent races, equally capable with our own of knowing and honouring the great Author of the universe ? Various writers have devoted many pages of ingenious speculation, and even separate works, to discussion of the probable characters, physical or moral, of the inhabitants of these sidereal worlds. But if it is certain that they are habitable, and probable that they are actually inhabited, can we believe that a mystery like that of the Incarnation should be wrought for our little planet alone, amidst thousands or millions of races, by which worlds on worlds may be peopled throughout the depths of infinite space?

This objection labours under one fatal defect, the entire want of all positive evidence in its favour. On the ground of a mere conjecture, which cannot be verified, it would set aside the central fact of a Divine revelation, attested by a large variety of concurrent evidence. It is argued that other suns and planets must be peopled with rational creatures, because otherwise the Creator would have been guilty of unwise profusion in forming such a multitude of worlds, either devoid of all inhabitants, or occupied by mere animals, that could render Him no worthy tribute of

praise. But if our judgment were not warped and moulded
by our own experience, surely the idea that rational creatures must needs be tied down in space to one sun or
planet, so as to be strictly inhabitants of one spot alone,
or else that the Creator would be robbed of all due praise
and worship, must be unnatural in the extreme. The
normal state of such a spirit is rather to be like the winds
of heaven, or the flames of fire, and free denizens of the
whole visible universe. To be tied down to one spot seems
more like a special humiliation and imprisonment than a
natural condition.

Again, the discoveries of geology, succeeding those of
astronomy, seem to reveal long ages of our earth's history,
before it was prepared and furnished to be the abode of
man. Whether, then, suns and planets were directly
created, or result from laws of material aggregation and
chemical change, the effects of which were foreseen and
foreordained by the Infinite Wisdom, it is most unlikely
that the time would be the same for all of them, in which
they became fit for the abode of an intelligent race. The
world which was first peopled, whichever it might be,
would be exposed to the illusion of supposing other worlds
to have reached already the same stage, and be equally
the dwelling of some other race of intelligent creatures
like its own.

Now since some world or other must probably be the
earliest peopled, and our earth seems to have been for long
ages entirely void of life, and then peopled only with its
lowest forms, before man appeared on it, the universe may
possibly be in the stage thus described. And even the
mere possibility that such is the case should restrain the
folly and license of speculation, when it would draw inferences from something entirely unknown, and on which

no grain of direct evidence exists, to destroy our faith in a Divine message, clearly and distinctly revealed. All that science can assure us of with regard to these starry worlds is that they form a vast and illimitable theatre, where, from ten thousand different centres, children of the dust, whether of our own race, or fashioned like ourselves, may perhaps hereafter be trained to enter on a still higher life of celestial happiness and glory.

Two races only of rational creatures, men and angels, are made known to us by any certain evidence. In each case the existence of the race is not more certain than the first entrance and present spread of moral evil. When we invent beautiful pictures of Arcadian innocence and simplicity in the system of Sirius or Arcturus, or the depths of the Milky Way, we may thus be overlooking very solemn lessons of daily experience or of direct revelation, which reveal the wide interval between defectible creatures and the Uncreated Goodness, and blot out from our own view some of the most humbling, but most profitable, truths in the whole compass of the revealed word of God. The vastness of creation may be made an excuse for shutting our eyes to the certainty of the fall of man, and our own condition as sinners, and to our need of the great redemption, wrought out for our fallen race through the condescending love and mercy of our Heavenly Father, and of the Only Begotten Son of God. Our wisdom is to cleave to certainties clearly revealed. Secret things belong to the Lord, but the things which are revealed to the sons of men, to give light to them in their present darkness, and to guide their feet into the way of peace.

CHAPTER XI.

ON THE NATURE OF THE ATONEMENT.

ATONEMENT by the sacrifice of Christ is the heart and life of Christianity. The Gospel rests upon the truth that "Christ died for our sins, according to the Scriptures," that He "was made a curse for us," and "bore our sins in his own body on the tree." But a clear apprehension of this great doctrine is a hard and high attainment, and no slight obscurity rests on it in many minds, which desire to hold it with a reasonable faith. Great questions arise, to which conflicting answers have been given. Did our Lord bear the sins of the saved only, or of all mankind? How far is the transfer of guilt to the innocent consistent with the eternal laws of truth and righteousness? Is the substitution total or partial? Does it include all sins, and sin in all aspects, or some only? What is the nature of the curse which Christ endured? What are the results of the sacrifice itself, and what are those which depend on the faith and repentance of the sinner? Is all punishment of those for whom an atonement has been made illegal and unjust? If Christ died for all, how is it that it is still "appointed for all men once to die"? Can the sentence be repealed by atonement, and still remain?

In the " Ways of God," chap. vii., I have attempted to throw some light on these difficulties. But the thoughts there published are too briefly expressed, and liable to misconstruction ; and have been approved by some, and condemned by others, on mistaken or insufficient grounds. A clearer exposition of them will, I trust, be a real help to many perplexed and thoughtful minds. Heresy itself is often the natural recoil from a distorted and lifeless orthodoxy. The moral government of God can hardly be subject to a worse travesty than when lowered to this one claim, that a certain amount of suffering must be exacted, it matters not from whom, for a certain number or amount of sins. The conscience revolts from a view so unworthy of the Divine holiness, so alien from the whole tenor of Divine revelation. A creed in which there is no substitution, and a creed in which there is nothing but substitution, depart equally, on opposite sides, from the truth of God. Let us try, with modesty and reverence, to disentangle, one by one, the difficulties in this part of revealed religion.

I. First, what is the extent of the atonement ? Did Christ die for the saved only, or for all mankind ?

Here the answer of the Bible is plain. There are texts where Christ is said to give himself for the Church, for his sheep. There are others where, indefinitely, He is said to die for many, for sinners, for men unjust. There are none where He is said to die for the Church only, for his sheep only. Such alone could exclude a wider message ; while these agree with it, and are included in it, as a part in the whole to which it belongs.

On the other hand, the language of many texts is strictly universal. "All we like sheep have gone astray; we have turned every one to his own way ; and the Lord

hath laid on him the iniquity of us all" (Isa. liii. 6).
"Behold the Lamb of God, which taketh away the sin
of the world" (John i. 29). "The bread I will give is
my flesh, which I will give for the life of the world"
(vi. 51). "If one died for all, then all died: and he died
for all, that they who live should not henceforth live to
themselves, but to him that died for them, and rose
again" (2 Cor. v. 14, 15). "God was in Christ, recon-
ciling the world unto himself" (v. 19). "That he, by
the grace of God, should taste death for every man"
(Heb. ii. 9). "Who gave himself a ransom for all"
(1 Tim. ii. 6). "And he is the propitiation for our sins;
and not for ours only, but for the sins of the whole world"
(1 John ii. 2). "We have seen, and do testify, that the
Father sent his Son to be the Saviour of the world"
(1 John iv. 14).

The same truth is implied in the very nature of the
Gospel. It calls on the sinner to believe what must be
true before he believes it, and this on the authority of
God's message, not of some secret hidden revelation to
himself alone. What he has first to believe is what the
Corinthians received first of all from the Apostle, that
Jesus Christ died for our sins (1 Cor. xv. 3). If He died
for the saved only, then the faith of the sinner, when he
first hears the Gospel, cannot rest on the simple word of
God. It must be builded rather on a secret persuasion
of his own final safety, for which that word, as yet, gives
him no warrant. None of the signs of grace, which it
supplies to the believer, can precede, but all must follow,
the first act by which he believes that Christ died for his
sins, and rests his hope on that atoning sacrifice.

The Church of England, in full harmony with Scripture, announces plainly the same truth, that Christ died

B.

M

for all men, and for all their sins. We read it in Art.
XXXI., in the summary of the Creed, in the Catechism,
and in the Communion doubly—both in the prayer of
consecration, and in the sublime thanksgiving near the
close. Thus it meets us in the first and the last steps of
that ladder of Jacob, by which babes and sucklings are
promoted into fellowship with the anthems and the worship of heaven.

II. Our Lord Jesus Christ, then, died for all. He
tasted death for every man. He is the propitiation, not
for Jews only, nor for believers only, but for the sins of
the whole world. And now the question must arise, Did
He die for multitudes wholly in vain ? Can sins be
atoned for, and the sinner still perish ? Can punishment be exacted from a Divine substitute, and those be
punished for whom this costly ransom has been paid ?
If the atonement includes all men, and still all men are
not saved, but many lost, must we not lower its efficacy,
and admit that, in many cases, Christ has died in vain ?
In what sense, then, can He have borne the sins of the
whole world ? What are the proper and direct results
of this atonement ? And what are those which flow
from it, but still depend on that moral change which is
wrought by the Gospel in the hearts of true penitents
alone ?

The answer to these questions must be sought in a
further truth. Christ bore indeed the sin of the world,
the collective guilt of all mankind. A truth how
strangely solemn, how sublimely glorious ! But all sin
has two different, almost opposite, characters. In one of
these it can, in the other it cannot, be transferred. It is
an act done once for all, which cannot be undone. Once
committed, it stands engraven on the scheme of Provi-

dence, a transgression of God's law, a rebellion against the Supreme Lawgiver, which needs some public vindication of his outraged authority. But it is also the act of a conscious agent, a sign of his present state, which may be changed or even reversed, but which, while it lasts, must make him hateful in the sight of a holy God.

Sin is a debt, and also a disease. It is a transgression of the Divine law, without and above the sinner. It is a transgression, also, against the health and life of the spirit within. Each view of it is equally Scriptural, equally important. The debt needs a ransom, the disease a cure. If sin were only a disease, there would be much room for sympathy, none for substitution. Atonement and propitiation would be wholly out of place. Our only want would be the healing, soothing power of some attractive pattern of perfect love. If sin were only a debt, substitution would be a complete Gospel, and all for whom an atonement was made would be heirs of salvation, because of that substitution alone. Those for whom Christ died would then be saved, even before they believe. Their debt once paid, no punishment or loss could reach them any more. Again, those who are not saved, on this view, must have had no sacrifice provided, no glad tidings sent. The Gospel, if preached to them at all, would only be a falsehood, a snare, and a delusion. They would be wholly beyond the redemption of Christ, like the fallen angels. The Saviour would neither have lived nor died for them, and to invite them to believe this would be simply persuading them to believe a lie.

These two aspects of sin, outwardly towards the law of God, and inwardly as the present sign of a state of heart displeasing to God, and ruinous to the soul's health, have an opposite relation to the doctrine of repentance. An act once done cannot be undone. No repentance can wipe out the stain, or reverse the record of rebellion. But sinful acts cease to be the index of a sinful heart, when the heart itself is changed by true repentance. The sinner then dies to the sin, and the sin itself expires in its character of a moral test. Thus the disease of sin needs to be healed by an inward work in the heart, and not by substitution. The debt may be borne and paid by a substitute, but can never be done away by repentance alone. So also, in actual life, a workman, disabled by grievous illness for his work, may contract a debt he cannot pay. He now suffers under a double burden—a debt unpaid, and a disease uncured. A physician might cure the complaint, but the debt would remain. A benefactor might pay the debt for him, and still the disease be unhealed. It is only a double gift, a payment and a cure, which can restore him to a state of freedom, health, and peace. And these two benefits might be linked with each other. If there is a medicine that can heal, and the sick man, through ignorance or prejudice, should refuse to apply it, he might be degraded into a helpless and worthless pauper, a mere drain on wasted benevolence, by help unwisely given. A wise benefactor might then make his promise to pay the debt already due to depend on proof of willingness to consult the physician, and use the prescribed remedies. The medicine would not pay the debt, nor the payment heal the disease; and still the payment and the first step in the cure would be linked inseparably in one work of love.

These two distinct aspects of all sin, when we look below the surface, enter into the whole economy of redemption, and even serve to define the very form of

Divine revelation. It consists of two distinct parts, the Law and the Gospel, the Old Covenant and the New. Again, the Law may be viewed in a double light, either as the earnest and preparation for the Gospel, containing all the germs of the later message, or else as its antithesis and contrast. The former aspect of the Law is unfolded in the Epistle to the Hebrews, and the latter, mainly, in those to the Galatians and the Romans.

What, then, is the nature of this contrast, which determines the whole structure of the word of God? The Law exhibits a perfect standard, and exacts a penalty for every failure. The Gospel assumes the moral bankruptcy of those to whom it is given, and provides a ransom for their guilt, and healing medicine for their moral and spiritual sickness. One deals with man as a creature, sets before him the rule of perfection, and severs all creatures into the unfallen and the fallen, the sinless and the sinful. The other deals with men as fallen creatures, sets before them a way of recovery, and severs them into the impenitent and the penitent, the faithless and the believing, those who still turn their backs upon the God of grace, and those who seek Him diligently, to regain his lost image in righteousness and true holiness. And thus the Law, as law, makes no provision for repentance. Its message is simple and solemn. "The soul that sinneth, it shall die." "Cursed is every one that continueth not in all things written in the book of the law, to do them." But it also recognizes the truth, that sin, though repentance cannot undo it, may be transferred from the sinner, and be the object of a Divinely-provided atonement. The Gospel reveals a true and Divine atonement, as the basis on which it wholly rests. But its own message, from the first, is a call to repentance, and a promise of forgiveness, adoption, and every blessing, to the penitent alone. It is the voice of the Law, that sin is a debt, a moral bankruptcy, a just exposure to death and the curse, which no mere repentance can do away, and which it needs a sin-offering to remove; and also that human help is vain, since "no man can redeem his brother, or give unto God a ransom for him." It is the voice of the Gospel, that a Divine atonement has been made, that Christ is "the Lamb of God, who taketh away the sin of the world;" and that an inward, personal change of heart, a present acceptance of God's mercy, a genuine faith in Christ, is the needful moral condition, that the disease of sin may be healed, and the sinner may be restored to the favour of God in this life, and the full enjoyment of his glorious presence in the life to come. The Law deals thus with all sin objectively, in reference to the strict claims of Divine justice, and the rights of the Supreme Lawgiver. The Gospel, first of all, reveals this claim as already satisfied by the death of Christ alone; and then deals with sin subjectively, in the actual rebellion of the heart, and brings the power of the Cross, and the energy of the quickening Spirit, to bear on these strongholds of the kingdom of darkness in the hearts of sinful men.

III. What, then, apart from the Atonement, is the state of mankind before God? What is their legal standing, and the nature of the curse and sentence under which they lie?

The Law of God is the standard of right and moral perfection. Its claim is unalterable, and cannot be lowered: perfect love to God, and love to man, and the actions that flow from perfect love. This is God's righteous claim, and, whenever it is not satisfied, the soul is morally bankrupt. Sin once committed, debt once incurred, can never be

cancelled by later obedience. That obedience is already
due, and its absence would be a new debt added to the
old. Thus, when sin has once entered, the Law, as law,
provides no remedy. Its promise is to the sinless alone.
To the sinful it denounces God's sentence—"The soul that
sinneth, it shall die."

The sentence of the broken law is death. But what is
the meaning of this death, the curse denounced by the
law on every transgressor? It needs some care and
thought to answer this question aright. The death meant
must be the same which was threatened in Paradise, and
which entered the world through Adam's sin. Again, it
is a contrast to the second death, the final sentence of the
last judgment. When one is inflicted, the other is abolished. "And death and hell were cast into the lake of
fire" (Rev. xx. 14). It is not the mere act of dying. In
all Scripture it is ascribed to the soul, even when separated
from the body. "In death there is no remembrance of
thee; and who will give thee thanks in the pit?" The
words temporal and eternal, often applied to death, tend
rather to mislead, than to explain the true nature
of this contrast. The first death is temporal, because its
future abolition is a revealed promise; but in its own
nature, apart from Christ's redemption, it would be everlasting. Neither the faculties of the creature, nor the
nature of sin, nor the justice of God, assign it any limit
or bound. It is due to a mighty work of redemption
alone, that it is swallowed up in eternal victory.

This death, the sentence of the law, extends to the
whole man, both soul and body. To see its nature as
respects the soul, we must reflect on its work with reference to the body. One is the visible sign and sacrament
of the other. The body is then parted from the soul, its

life; and being thus parted, becomes the prey of inward corruption. So, also, death is the separation of the soul from God, the true source of life; and all the confusion, chaos, and moral corruption and dissolution which follows that awful separation. Without, there is banishment from the presence of God, and from all the light of his favour and blessing. Within, there will follow the unrestrained working of moral corruption, degrading, perverting, desecrating all the faculties and powers of the immortal spirit. Sin would thus become, under the name of death, a "finished" evil, its own ever-growing torment, and the soul sink deeper and deeper in an abyss of hopeless misery.

On this view we may see the force of the contrasted figures, by which the first and second death are portrayed. One is "the lake of fire," solemn indeed and most awful, yet bounded in its range, shut in by firm land on every side. The other is "the deep," the abyss, "the bottomless pit," evil reigning, rioting, growing, deepening without limit and without end, in its fatal descent, farther and farther, from light, happiness, and heaven. By the sentence of the law, fulfilled without atonement or redemption, mankind, once fallen, would be shut out from God's presence, and sink and sink, and sink for ever, in this abyss of hopeless and endless ruin. There would have been, through ages without end, the awful reality of a God-dishonouring, God-hating, God-blaspheming, self-tormenting, God-abandoned universe. Such death is the wages of sin, its due desert, and the issue to which it naturally tends. It is the fatal harvest from the seeds of moral corruption harboured in the soul. "Sin, when it is finished, bringeth forth death."

IV. What, now, is the nature of Christ's Atonement?

What is the curse He endured for sin? What is the direct and proper result of that Atonement, apart from the mighty moral change, in all who obey the Gospel, wrought by the magnetic, transforming power of the Cross of Christ?

Here the testimony of Scripture is plain. "The Lord hath laid on him the iniquity of us all." "He made him to be sin for us, who knew no sin." "Christ hath redeemed us from the curse of the law, being made a curse for us." "He suffered for our sins, the just for the unjust." "Who himself bore our sins in his own body on the tree." "Behold the Lamb of God, which taketh away the sin of the world." A sinful character was never once ascribed to our Lord. He was, and was ever held to be, in the midst of his sufferings, the Holy One of God, who might not see corruption, the Lamb of God without blemish or spot, who "knew no sin." Sin was ascribed or imputed to Him, not as the sign of a sinful character, but in direct contrast to the claims of a character declared to be free from all spot or stain of sin. It was in its other aspect, as a series of acts done, that could not be reversed, of transgressions against the authority of the Supreme Lawgiver, that the sin of the world, one vast collective whole, was laid, like the wood of the sacrifice, upon the shoulders of the world's Redeemer. And the curse which He bore was death, the first death, so far as it was due to the demerit of sin and the claims of Divine justice alone, and was not aggravated by the further working of moral corruption in the heart of God-abandoned sinners.

When God reveals his justice in dealing with the moral character of men, He must deal with them according to the truth. The Holy One, who loved righteousness and hated iniquity, whose life was sinless, and whose love is perfect, must then be anointed with the oil of gladness above his fellows. But when He deals with sin in its other aspect, as transgression of the law, reversible by no repentance, the perfection of the Victim on whom the guilt is laid, and from whom the penalty is exacted, serves only to place in the clearest light the essential sinfulness and hatefulness of sin, and the authority of that law which the sinner has despised. The claim of God's holiness is ill explained by a law of mechanical compensation, as if the sufferings, for a few days and nights, of an Infinite Person, were exactly equal to those of the multitudes of mankind through a whole eternity of ruin and sorrow. Sin and its punishment are not such finite, measurable things. What is needed for the full vindication of God's authority is that his holy anger against all sin, as sin, should, once for all, be displayed to the uttermost, before any soul that has fallen from God, and rebelled against Him, can be restored to the perfect enjoyment of his favour and blessing. This is the baptism of fire, of which our Lord said, " How am I straitened, till it be accomplished ! " He endured for our sakes that death which is the curse of the broken law, and in his case its sting was not removed. He cried upon the cross, " My God, my God, why hast thou forsaken me ? " He suffered the pains, the pangs of death. He was laid " in the lowest pit, in darkness, in the deeps," and was vexed with all the storms and waves of God's holy displeasure against the sin of a guilty world. The Highest and the Holiest stooped to the lowest abasement of shame and sorrow. He endured death, the sentence of the Law in all its darkest terrors, so far as these are separable from the aggravations caused by reigning sin, gloomy remorse, fierce, untamed passion, deep self-torment, and utter despair.

When once this claim of Divine justice against sin, as sin, had thus been fully satisfied, and the Holy One had descended to the deep of Sheol, enduring the bitter anguish of sojourn in the dark land of death, then the further claim of the same justice, that all shall be dealt with according to their true moral character, began forthwith to assert its unchangeable authority. The pains of death were loosed, because it was not possible that the Sinless One should be holden thereby. No sooner had He entered the deep, fathomed its dark abyss, and endured the worst extreme of separation from his heavenly Father, than the curse exhausted its bitterness, and the blessing began to reveal its power. That same day He left the deep of Sheol or Hades, and entered its Paradise, the sheltered resting-place of the faithful dead. The third day He left the under-world of the dead, and rose victorious from the grave, to die no more. The fortieth day He completed his upward return, and "journeyed into heaven, angels, and authorities, and powers being made subject unto him." Because He had stooped unutterably low, He was raised unutterably high, "far above all principality, and power, and might, and every name that is named, not only in this world, but in the world to come."

The direct and immediate result of this great atonement answers to its character, as thus defined, and is clearly pointed out in the word of God. The world is now reconciled to God. Rom. xi. 15. 2 Cor. v. 19. The veil of the law's condemnation, spread over the face of all nations, is taken away and destroyed. Isa. xxv. 7. No amount of past sin is now any barrier to the instant restoration of the sinner to God's favour and blessing. The middle wall of partition, which no bitter repentance could remove, is broken down, and there is free and instant access for every returning penitent to the house and home of love, from which their sins had banished them. There is left no hindrance, no barrier without, on the part of Divine justice, administering a perfect Law; but only the hindrance within, from the present unbelief and pride of those who will not accept a Divine remedy, and who resist and cast aside the grace of the Gospel. The curse and condemnation of the Law is done away in the cross of Christ. The condemnation of the Gospel alone remains. "And this is the condemnation, that light is come into the world, and men loved darkness rather than light, because their deeds were evil." And thus the effects of Christ's Atonement, common to all mankind, are these: the removal of an impassable and hopeless barrier between sinful creatures and a holy God; the provision of a day of grace, in which mercy may be found; rich forbearance and long-suffering towards years and ages of abounding sin; the abolition of the first death, the wages of sin, which is to be swallowed up in eternal victory; the resurrection of the body; and the transfer of men from the reign of death, and the curse of utter vanity, to a state in which God, the God of love and holiness, will be for ever glorified—though by some in the height of heavenly glory, and by others only in the depth of just retribution and eternal shame.

V. What, in the last place, is the connection between the Atonement and the special benefits obtained by those who believe and obey the Gospel?

Sin is both a debt and a disease. It is doubly a debt, both directly, as a transgression, or series of transgressions of God's law; and indirectly, as the sign of a rebellious state of heart, involving guilt as well as corruption before God. The Atonement, in itself, removes the debt only, and in its first and simplest aspect alone. But the guilt of present rebellion, and the disease of reigning sin, can be removed only by an inward change of heart, the work of the regenerating Spirit of God. Here the Atonement avails, not by the mere fact of its accomplishment on the cross, but as a moral magnet, a mighty fountain of new and heavenly life to the souls of men. The substitution of Christ belongs to his sacrificial death alone. But his incarnation, his sinless life, his glorious resurrection and ascension, are all equally the source of those gifts which, as the federal head of mankind, and more especially of the Church, He pours down abundantly upon all his people. He bore the curse of the Law, that men might not bear it. He died, that men might not taste of death in its full bitterness, armed with its deadly sting, nor remain under its power, but that it might be destroyed for ever. But He stooped from heaven, that He might raise us to heaven. He obeyed, that we too might obey. He humbled himself that He might make us humble. He rose from the dead, that we too might rise. He ascended, as our Forerunner, that in due season we also might ascend, and sit with Him in heavenly places in the world to come. In these aspects of his redeeming work, substitution has no place, but federal headship alone. The Atonement prepares the way for these further benefits. It is the only foundation on which they rest. But it does not secure them by the mere fact that a full sacrifice has been made. They depend on a further work of repentance and faith in the heart of the sinner, whereby the soul is engrafted into the true Vine, and becomes a living member of the mystical body of Christ. Till this change is wrought, the curse of the Law is removed, but the curse of the Gospel remains. "He that believeth not is condemned already, because he hath not believed in the name of the only begotten

Son of God." And the disease of sin also remains still without a cure. The rebellion is even aggravated by the greatness of the mercy which is still despised, and the rich provision of grace, which the soul refuses to receive. But the same Atonement, which removes the legal curse, is the grand instrument appointed by God, and applied and used by the Holy Spirit, for working this inward and mighty change in the hearts of men.

When a rich and kind friend pays a debt for a prisoner, the substitution properly belongs to the payment only, and its immediate effect is his immediate release from prison. But the same friend, when the debtor is released, may receive him into his family, provide him with a fresh education, and introduce him into a new sphere of life, leading to riches, happiness, and honour. The prisoner, condemned before to the society of criminals, and sinking fast in moral degradation, may come under better and nobler influences; and gratitude for the benefit he has received may lead him to copy the moral excellences of the beloved benefactor, by whom his ransom was paid, and on whom all his present comforts and blessings depend. All these results are no part of the payment which was first made. No law of justice requires that they should exactly equal that sacrifice of comfort or ease to which the rich friend submitted on his payment of the debt. And yet they are so entirely dependent on this first act of love, that, in a looser sense, they may be called the purchase of that first ransom. In strictness of speech, however, this phrase does not apply, and rather tends to obscure the true nature and condition of these latter benefits. And thus we find in the Scriptures that Christ is never said to have bought blessings for His people: nor are adoption, regeneration, holiness, peace, resurrection, ever styled the purchase of his pre-

cious blood. It is his people themselves who are pur-
chased, bought, redeemed from the power of the curse, the
bondage of sin, the dominion of Satan ; that being brought
out of the prison-house, and made once more the freemen
of the Lord, they may freely receive, with no impediment
from Divine justice, whatever blessings the free bounty of
God the Father is pleased to bestow. And yet all these
gifts and blessings come to them through Christ alone.
He is the Vine, and they are the branches. He is the
Head, and they are the members. He is the great Fountain, from whom and through whom alone every stream
of grace must flow down to a sinful world. Spiritual
union with the risen Saviour is the fixed, unalterable
condition on which all the blessings of personal salvation
must for ever depend.

The curse of the Law can be removed by the Atonement alone, believed or disbelieved. The curse of the
Gospel, the moral guiltiness of present rebellion, the sore
sickness and disease of indwelling sin, can be removed
by repentance and faith alone, and in no other way.
Here substitution can have no place. Each must repent
for himself. Each must believe for himself. Each for
himself must lay hold upon the promises of the new
covenant. To bear the burdens of others is the law of
Christ, which finds its highest fulfilment in his atoning
sacrifice alone. But this work of the Redeemer in our
stead must be followed by a work of the Holy Spirit within us, in which the spirit of man is a fellow-worker with
God, before salvation can be ours in the fulness of its
revealed blessings. And here the further truth applies,
that " every man shall bear his own burden." " He that
soweth to the flesh shall of the flesh reap corruption ; but
he that soweth to the Spirit shall of the Spirit reap life

everlasting." A great work of Divine love has been
wrought for mankind, once for all, upon the cross, whereby
the first death has been abolished, and will be swallowed
up in eternal victory. But a further work is needful,
wrought by the Spirit of God in every contrite heart,
through faith in that Divine atonement; that the soul
may attain a full salvation, and being freed from the
power of the second death, may have right to the tree
of life, and enter in through the gates into the celestial
city.

CHAPTER XII.

ON ETERNAL JUDGMENT.

THE doctrine of Eternal Punishment is the most solemn of all those revealed in the word of God. It has awakened deep repugnance and antipathy not only from the openly unbelieving and profane, but from many who may claim the character of pious and devoted Christians. Many accept it, in submission to what appears to them the plain testimony of the Scriptures, but with much inward perplexity and distress of mind. Others cherish the hope, which they hardly venture openly to profess, that the Church on this point has failed to expound the warnings of God's word aright, and that its solemn threatenings are either conditional, and may never be realised through some act of Divine mercy and omnipotence, or temporary, so as to be followed either by restoration to holiness and happiness, or by an utter extinction of being. The various alternatives proposed exclude and contradict each other. They agree only in the common principle that the eternal punishment of a large proportion, if not the great majority, of the human race, is a tenet so awful and overwhelming in its nature, that scarcely any evidence is sufficient to establish its truth. I shall propose, first, to inquire directly what is the real testimony of the word of God, and next, to consider whether the moral difficulties, alleged to rest upon the common faith of Christians, may not be lightened or removed by other truths, inwrought into the whole texture of the word of God. May He who is the God of love and holiness, and the Fountain of all wisdom, enable me to treat the subject with due reverence, and to give some help to those whose spirits have been perplexed or overwhelmed by meditation on this solemn aspect of divine revelation.

The passages of the New Testament in which future punishment is spoken of, and either its reality, its severity, or its continuance affirmed, are these: Mat. iii. 10, 12, v. 21, 22, 26, 29, 30, vii. 13, 14, 23, viii. 12, 29, x. 28, 39, xi. 22, 24, xii. 31, 32, xiii. 30, 41, 42, 48, 50, xvi. 26, xviii. 8, 9, 34, 35, xxii. 12—14, xxiii. 14, 33, xxv. 41, 46, xxvi. 24; Mar. iii. 28—30, vi. 11, viii. 35—38, ix. 43—48, xvi. 16; Lu. xii. 4, 5, 10, xvi. 19—31; Joh. iii. 15, 16, 36, v. 29, viii. 24; Acts i. 25; Rom. i. 18, ii. 5, 16, ix. 22; 1 Cor. i. 18, iii. 13, 15; Phil. i. 28, iii. 19 ; 1 Th. i. 10, v. 3; 2 Th. i. 7—9, ii. 10; 1 Ti. vi. 9; Heb. ii. 3, vi. 8, x. 26—39, xii. 25, 29; Ja. ii. 13, v. 20; 1 Pet. iv. 17, 18; 2 Pet. ii. 9, 17, 21, iii. 7, 16; 1 Jo. v. 16; Ju. 13; Rev. ii. 11, xiv. 9—11, xix. 3, xx. 6, 10, 11, 15, xxi. 5—8, xxii. 11, 12, 18.   These texts, and some hundred others in the Old Testament, when read with care, and compared together, have been felt by most Christians to contain these doctrines, as revealed truths of God; that there is a life after death, and a judgment to come ; that this judgment includes the acceptance of the righteous, and the public condemnation of the unrighteous and unholy; that their existence does not cease, either at death or the resurrection, but lasts for ever; and that the sentence upon them is never to be annulled or reversed, but is to be an eternal manifestation of the evil of sin, and the righteous anger of a holy God; and that their doom is one of anguish and sorrow without end. Or in the words of Christ himself, "that their worm dieth not, and their fire is not quenched," but their punishment lasts for evermore.

This awakening and solemn message of eternal judgment does not depend on these texts alone. It seems really inwrought into the whole texture of the word of God. It results from the combination of four separate truths, which pervade the whole course and series of God's messages to mankind.

The first of these is the fundamental contrast in the moral condition of men, even in the present life. "All have sinned and come short of the glory of God." In this common character of men, as sinful and fallen, "there is no difference," Rom. iii. 22, 23. "There is not a just man on earth, that liveth, and sinneth not," Eccl. vii. 20. But still there is, in God's sight, an entire contrast between the state of penitent and impenitent sinners, of believers and unbelievers, of those who forsake and turn away from their sins, and those who abide under the power of rebellion and iniquity. These two classes are set before us under a large variety of names, but in constant opposition to each other. They are called variously the righteous and the wicked, the just and the unjust, the holy and the unholy, the meek and lowly in heart, and the proud and haughty, those who fear God, and those who fear Him not, the faithful and the unfaithful, wheat and chaff, wheat and tares, the seed of the woman and the seed of the serpent, the children of God, and children of the devil. This contrast meets us in all the histories of Scripture from first to last, from the death of righteous Abel, and the saving of righteous Noah in the ark, when the flood came on the world of the ungodly, to the descriptions of moral conflict

between ungodly rulers and people, and the followers of
the Lamb, called and chosen and faithful, in the latest
prophecy of the word of God.   No truth, perhaps, has a
greater amount of Scripture testimony, than this doctrine
of a fundamental contrast in the present moral condition
of men.   And the main scope of the Gospel is to invite
those who are now careless and disobedient to repent and
turn to God, and to do works meet for repentance, that
they may be delivered from the wrath to come, and which
rests, even now, on the unbelieving and the profane.

The second great truth is that death is not the end of
human existence.   One main element of the faith of the
Gospel is "the resurrection of the dead, and the life of the
world to come."   This great doctrine of a further and continued life of men after what we call death is taught in
many places of the Old Testament, so that the Sadducees,
in denying it, erred, not knowing the Scriptures; but much
more plainly and fully in the New Testament.   Many
passages affirm or imply the continued existence of the
soul, after the death of the body, when it is consigned to
the grave; but the clearest and fullest affirmation of it is
given in the great doctrine of the resurrection.   "As in
Adam all die, even so in Christ shall all be made alive."
"We must all appear before the judgment seat of Christ,
that every one may receive the things done in his body,
according to that he hath done, whether it be good or bad."
This doctrine that "it is appointed to all men once to die,
but after this the judgment" was revealed gradually, under
the law and the prophets, with growing clearness, but was
brought most fully to light by the Gospel, and its message
of the resurrection of Christ, and his future return in
glory, to be the Judge of both the living and the dead.

A third truth follows, in agreement with the two others.

The present moral contrast, in God's sight, will have its issue hereafter in a like contrast in the Divine sentence pronounced on sinners in the great day of account. Some will be justified, others will be condemned. Some will be heirs of salvation, others will be visited with destruction. Some, like wheat, will be gathered into the garner; others, like chaff or tares, will be burned with fire. Some will be placed, like sheep, at the right hand of the Judge, and receive a sentence of blessing; others, as the goats, will be placed at the left hand, and hear from his lips the awful sentence, Depart from me, ye cursed. Those who have sown to the flesh will of the flesh reap corruption; while those who have sown to the Spirit, shall of the Spirit reap life everlasting. The contrast of reward and punishment in the judgment to come is repeated many times, and forms one main feature in the Psalms and later Prophets, and the whole of the New Testament. It is conspicuous alike in the last chapter of both. "For behold, the day cometh that shall burn as an oven; and all the proud, yea, and all that do wickedly, shall be as stubble, and the day that cometh shall burn them up, saith the Lord of hosts, that it shall leave them neither root nor branch. But unto you that fear my name shall the Sun of righteousness arise, with healing in his wings." And again, "Blessed are they that do his commandments, that they may have right to the tree of life, and enter in through the gates into the city. For without are dogs, and sorcerers, and whoremongers, and murderers, and idolaters, and whosoever loveth and maketh a lie."

Fourthly, the nature of this judgment, whether in reward or punishment, is not temporary and transient, but abiding and eternal. "He that blasphemeth against the Holy Ghost hath never forgiveness, but is in danger of

eternal damnation." "Verily I say unto thee, Thou shalt
by no means come out thence, till thou hast paid the
uttermost farthing." "These shall go away into everlasting
punishment, but the righteous into life everlasting."
"Who shall be punished with everlasting destruction from
the presence of the Lord, and from the glory of his power."
To the presumptuous and self-willed, who are not afraid to
blaspheme dignities, who walk after the flesh in the lust
of uncleanness, "the mist of darkness is reserved for ever."
They are "wandering stars, to whom is reserved the blackness of darkness for ever." Among the first principles and
foundations of the Gospel is the doctrine "of the resurrection of the dead, and of eternal judgment," Heb. vi. 2.
And in the book of Revelation, the crown and close of the
messages of God, the same phrase is used three times to
denote the continuance of future punishment (Rev. xiv.
11, xix. 3, xx. 10), which is also used nine times to express
the duration of God's own existence and dominion, Rev. i.
6, iv. 9, 10, v. 13, 14, vii. 12, x. 6, xi. 15, xv. 7, and once
also for the continued blessedness of the redeemed, xxii. 5.

The rejection of this doctrine admits of three varieties,
inconsistent with each other, and each of them loaded with
difficulties of its own. The first is the doctrine that death
is the extinction of being to the ungodly, so that a future
life of any kind is limited to the faithful. The second is
the view that æonian punishment is not eternal, but that
a long period of severe suffering, after the resurrection, is
then followed by utter extinction and loss of being. The
third is the creed of universalism, or that after a season of
punishment, wicked men and angels are all finally restored to the Divine favour and blessing, and share, perhaps with some difference of degree, in the bliss of the
redeemed.

The first of these views is directly opposed to all those passages, which speak of the continued existence of evil men, after their bodily death, and to those, if possible still plainer, which distinctly affirm a resurrection of the unjust as well as the just. A being which is wholly extinct cannot be revived. It would be the creation of a new and different being. The revealed truth of the resurrection of the dead wholly excludes the notion that death is, in the case of men, an entire annihilation or destruction of the individual being.

If death meant ceasing to exist at all, there could be no resurrection of the dead, but only a creation of new beings, to replace others which had wholly perished. There could also be no possibility of a second death, if the meaning of death were an entire abolition of the individual being. For this plainly could occur only once for all, and never be repeated. This first of the three substitutes for the usual faith of Christians is therefore most plainly opposed to the whole series of Scripture statements with regard to the survival of the spirit, when the body has crumbled to the dust, the resurrection both of the just and the unjust, and description of the doom of the ungodly as the second death.

The second and third opinions admit a coming resurrection of all the dead, whether righteous or unrighteous, and the continued existence of their souls, when separated from the body. They agree, further, in recognizing, as a revealed truth, a long or age-lasting season of suffering and penal infliction to the ungodly. They alike affirm that this punishment is not strictly eternal or without end, but comes at length to a close. They diverge as to what then ensues. One class holds that the being of sinners is burnt up and destroyed by the severity of their sufferings, so that they are utterly extinguished, and cease to exist. The others hold that their sufferings are like a purgatorial fire, and that they are afterwards recovered to share eternally in the bliss of the redeemed.

But this construction of the word "everlasting" in Matt. xxv. 41, 46, 2 Th. i. 9, and of "for ever and ever" in Rev. xiv. 11, xix. 3, xx. 10, to denote an age or season, which comes to an end, when it is used in the same verses to express the eternal felicity of the redeemed, and in the same context to describe God's own eternal being, is most forced and unnatural. The word $αἰώνιος$ occurs more than seventy times in the New Testament. Seven of these refer to future punishment, everlasting fire, destruction or judgment, Matt. xviii. 8, xxv. 41, 46, Mark iii. 29, 2 Th. i. 9, Heb. vi. 2, Jude 7. All the rest, with three exceptions, Rom. xvi. 25, 2 Tim. i. 9, Tit. i. 2, refer either to the duration of the future bliss of the redeemed, or to the Divine eternity. And in these three exceptions the plural form, and the association with $χρόνος$, evidently require a partial modification of the strict and usual meaning. They refer not to the future but the past, those birth-ages of the world which lose themselves in the abyss of the Divine eternity. As applied to the future, the usage is unbroken, and the word is constantly employed to denote that which has no termination. The only text where a doubt could arise is Rev. xiv. 6, where the angel is said to preach "the everlasting gospel" to every kindred on the face of the earth. And this most naturally denotes a message of glad tidings, not limited to this mortal life, but reaching onward to eternity.

But if the construction of these texts, required in common by both forms of the doctrine, which denies eternal punishment, is unnatural and untenable, each is pressed by separate difficulties, where they diverge from each other. And first, the doctrine of annihilation or destruction supposes that all the ungodly survive the death of the body, most of them for hundreds or thousands of years, that they are afterward raised from the dead, that in resurrection-bodies they hear and undergo the sentence of the Righteous Judge, that they are tormented with fire and flame for long ages, and then at last their very being is blotted out and extinguished, like chaff which wholly disappears when burnt, and leaves not a trace behind. This view, of course, must abandon every argument based on the assertion that death and destruction mean annihilation. For on this theory all those who die, are lost, or destroyed, do not cease to exist, but first abide in Hades, awaiting the resurrection, and then continue to exist in bodies of the resurrection, for long ages, enduring a penal sentence from God. It is self evident that the words death, the loss of the soul, or destruction, are applied only to the first death, or dissolution of the body, or the state of a soul that still exists, when the day of grace has ended, or to the sentence which casts into outer darkness or the lake of fire. The awful name of " the second death " is not applied to some point of time, conjectured, not revealed, when penal suffering comes to an end by the guilty soul ceasing to exist, but to that state of penal suffering itself. To be cast into the lake of fire is the second death.

But while the admission of the double truth, that the ungodly are raised from the dead, and suffer in the body, at least for a long season, a penal sentence, sets aside every argument, which assumes that death and destruction mean the end of conscious existence, this involves moral and metaphysical difficulties of the gravest kind.

The gifts and calling of God are "without repentance". If then a conscious being, not dependent on bodily organs, and fitted in itself to endure for ever, has been given, and should afterwards be withdrawn, this would seem to reverse a great law of God's moral government. If, to avoid this difficulty, we look upon consciousness as depending on the compound nature of the soul, so that it can be resolved into unconscious elements, the difficulty is increased on the other side. Such a view is simple materialism, and involves a denial of man's responsibility as a personal and individual being.

Again, if later extinction of men's spiritual being were granted to be possible in itself, the revealed fact of the resurrection must render it highly unnatural and improbable. A great and miraculous work of Divine power would thus have been wrought, only to be reversed once more. It is hard to conceive of the work of creation as reversed by utter extinction. But that a being, half extinguished, and buried in the land of darkness, should be brought into the full possession of natural powers, once suspended, and the light of manifest judgment, only to be reduced again to utter nothingness, and sink into a more total darkness than before, seems like a strange vacillation, quite unworthy of Him who is perfect in wisdom. If God's work, in the creation of men and angels, is the irreversible gift of an intelligent and responsible being, and this "without repentance," or incapable of being withdrawn, consistently with the perfections of God, we may then see a clear reason for the fact of the resurrection, both of the just and the unjust. In all his creatures God must be glorified, however strange and solemn the forms which, in some cases, this great truth may assume. But if souls are perishable as to their natural existence, and may be reduced to nothing, it is hard to imagine any reason for protracted torture of the rebellious, instead of cutting short the duration of evil, and blotting them out at once, without delay, from the universe of God.

It is claimed for this view, that, in contrast with the usual doctrine, it maintains the non-eternity of evil. But it seems to me that exactly the reverse is true. Evil is not abolished, if the All-wise Creator is obliged to undo in part his own work of creation, and destroy multitudes of his creatures, the noblest and highest in their natural powers, because He cannot find means whereby to glorify himself in their continued being. The principle is the same as in the wider hypothesis, that God should abstain from creation altogether, through a foresight of the moral evils that would ensue from the existence of mutable and responsible creatures. In this case, as I have said before, evil would achieve its most fatal and awful triumph, by planting its victorious standard within the citadel of moral perfection and goodness, and turning the Fountain of living waters into a dull marsh, from which no stream of grace and blessing should ever flow. The same reasons which forbid the Infinitely Wise to forbear creation, through fear of the evils sin would introduce into his universe, equally forbid the total destruction of any of his creatures, fitted by their creation to enjoy life for ever, because He is not able, through their sin and rebellion, to glorify himself in them in any other way.

Let us now consider the other alternative. It admits, in deference to the express words of Scripture, a long lasting punishment of those who die without having embraced the offered grace of the gospel. It agrees with the destructionist creed that this period, however long it may be, will come to an end. But it diverges from it in maintaining that the later result is not utter extinction, but restoration to happiness and the Divine favour. The contrast comes to be, not between the saved and the lost, but between those who are saved through the sufferings of Christ, and others who are saved through penal anguish, sorrow, and fiery vengeance upon sin, which they themselves have endured in their own persons.

Does this doctrine of universal restoration, and a common and equal salvation to be enjoyed, with a difference in the date alone, by those who have lived and died in faith and in unbelief, agree with the plain unforced teaching of the word of God ? I cannot, for myself, understand how any honest and simple readers of the Bible, however deep their shrinking from the doctrine of eternal punishment, can accept such a view as the real testimony of the inspired Scriptures. The contrast of present moral state and future doom between two opposite classes of men, the just and the unjust, the holy and the unholy, believers and unbelievers, the humble and the proud, those who fear God and who fear Him not, the penitent and the impenitent, those who confess their guilt before the Most High and forsake it, and those who cover and conceal it, and refuse to let it go, seems one of the most central and vital truths in all the messages of God's word from first to last. On this contrast it is that all the warnings of God's Law and the promises of the Gospel alike depend. From the first sentence on the Serpent, " I will put enmity between thee and the woman, between thy seed and her seed," onward through the histories of Cain and Abel, of Noah and the world of the ungodly, of Abraham and his intercession for Sodom, and Israel in the wilderness, to the warning, at the close of Malachi, of the day that will burn as an oven, and the rising of the Sun of righteousness with healing in his wings; and again, from the mention of the wheat and chaff, of the strait and wide gate, the narrow and the broad way, the wedding guests and the man without a wedding garment, the wise virgins and the foolish, the sheep and the goats, in St Matthew's Gospel, the great gulf fixed between Lazarus and the rich man in the Gospel of St Luke, and onward to the very close of the New Testament, the same contrast meets us in almost every page. The purpose of the Gospel is to turn men "from darkness to light, and from the power of Satan to God, that they may receive forgiveness of their sins, and an inheritance among them that are sanctified." Its actual reception answers ever to those words at the close of Acts—"Some believed the things which were spoken, and some believed not." And the final result is expressed or implied in that parting message of the Son of God, which announces the present forbearance or time of probation, and the sequent judgment—"He that is unjust, let him be unjust still; and he that is filthy, let him be filthy still; and he that is righteous, let him be righteous still, and he that is holy, let him be holy still. And behold I come quickly, and my reward is with me, to give every man according as his work shall be."

The doctrine of universalism seems thus to nullify and set aside one of the most fundamental and pervasive truths in the whole compass of Divine revelation. All the exhortations, warnings, invitations, and appeals of the Gospel, rest upon the revealed fact, that this life is a season of probation, and that on the present acceptance or rejection of the offered grace of God, eternal results depend; namely, a contrast of acceptance or rejection, of reward or punishment, in that great day when the secrets of all hearts shall be revealed. To contradict and reject this solemn truth is really to break one of the two main-springs of the Gospel, and abolishes one chief element of its double appeal, by hope and by fear, in promises of salvation, and warnings of certain judgment, to the hearts and consciences of men.

The statements, then, in the next chapter, are not designed to contradict or set aside that doctrine of a future punishment of the unbelieving and the ungodly, never to end, which I believe, and have always believed, since I first meditated closely on this solemn subject, to be distinctly revealed. My starting-point, in my earlier treatment of it, was an express adoption of the words of a correspondent, who sought for relief from his inward perplexities, that "nothing can be more positively laid down by our Lord, than that the reward of heaven and the punishment of hell are eternal, and strange warnings of judgment to come pervade almost every page." The same conviction remains unchanged, after a perusal of much that has been written on the other side. Death is not a cessation of existence, else there could be no resurrection of the dead, and no second death. All are not to be saved alike, for the most conspicuous truth in the warnings and promises of Scripture is the contrast between those who are saved and those who perish, and who perish, not by a total extinction of being, but by enduring for ever a solemn sentence of eternal judgment.

CHAPTER XIII.

OBJECTIONS AND EXPLANATIONS.

THE doctrine of judgment to come, as taught in Scripture, has not only caused deep inward perplexity to many devout minds, but has been turned by multitudes into an excuse for their entire rejection of the Bible as a supernatural and inspired message. Perfect love seems to imply a sincere desire for the happiness of every conscious and intelligent creature. A perfect victory of almighty love seems further to require that this desire for the happiness of others shall not fail and be frustrate in any case by the strength of evil, but that it shall be at length fulfilled. Here, then, at first sight there is a direct contradiction between express and repeated statements of Scripture, and natural and almost inevitable inferences from those moral perfections of God, which are shown dimly by the light of nature, but have been most clearly and abundantly revealed in the word of God. No wonder, then, that many Christians still feel great inward perplexity, when their thoughts turn to this solemn subject, the future doom of the wicked, and that unbelievers and half-believers should inveigh loudly against the common view of Christian believers, as an unreasonable and gloomy superstition.

Let us listen first to Theodore Parker, a favourite author, some years ago, with young Hindoos who had broken loose from their native superstitions, while still adversaries to Christian Faith. In his *Discourses on Absolute Religion* he declaims against the grand and striking narrative of Num. xiv., on the report of the spies, the rebellion of the people, and the intercession of Moses, in these frightful terms :

" If an unprejudiced Christian were to read this for the first time in a heathen writer, and it was related of Kronos or Moloch, he would say—What foul ideas these heathen have of God ! thank heaven, we are Christians, and cannot believe in a Deity so terrible ! Is God angry with men, passionate, revengeful, offended because they will not war and butcher the innocent ? Would he violate his holy law, by a miracle to destroy a whole nation, millions of men, women and children, because they fall into a natural fit of despair, and refuse to trust two rather than ten witnesses ? Does God require men's words to restrain his rage, violence, and a degree of fury, which Nero and Caracalla, butchers as they were, would have shuddered to think of ? Is he to be teazed and coaxed from murder ? Are we to believe this in the name of Christianity ? Then perish Christianity from the face of the earth, and let man learn of his religion and of his God from the stars and the violets, the lion and the lamb ! There are some things which may be true, but must be rejected for lack of evidence ; but this story no amount of evidence could make possible."

The supposed views of ordinary Protestant Christians as to the future sentence on the ungodly are portrayed in a similar tone, in these words :

" The saints and martyrs, who bore trials in the world,

are to take their vengeance by shouting Hallelujah, when they see the anguish of their old persecutors, and the smoke of their torment ascending for ever and ever. Do the joys of Paradise pall on the senses of the elect ? They look off in the distance to the tortures of the damned, where destruction is naked before them, and hell hath no covering ; where the devil stirreth up the embers of the fire that is never quenched ; where the doubters, whom the church could neither answer nor put to silence, the great men of antiquity, the men great, gifted, and glorious, who mocked at difficulty, softened the mountains of despair, and hewed a path amid the trackless waste, that mortal feet might tread the way of peace ; where the great men of modern times, who would not insult the Deity by bowing to the foolish word of a hireling priest ; where all these writhe in their torture, turn and turn, but find no ray, but yell in fathomless despair ; and when the elect behold all this, they say, striking on their harps of gold, Aha! we are comforted, and thou art tormented ; for the Lord God omnipotent reigneth, and our garments are washed white in the blood of the Lamb." (pp. 248, 346.)

Mr Lecky, in his able *History of European Morals*, touches on the same subject, and writes as follows:

"That an all-righteous and all-merciful Creator, in the full exercise of those attributes, deliberately calls into existence sentient beings, whom He has from eternity irrevocably destined to endless, unspeakable, unmitigated torture, is a proposition at once so extravagantly absurd, and so ineffably atrocious, that its adoption might well lead men to doubt the universality of moral perceptions. Such teaching is, in fact, simply dæmonism, and dæmonism in its most extreme form. It ascribes to the Creator acts of injustice and cruelty, which it would be absolutely im-

B.   O

possible for the imagination to surpass, before which the
most monstrous excesses of human cruelty dwindle into
insignificance; acts, in fact, considerably worse than any
which theologians have attributed to the devil. If there
were men who, while vividly realizing the nature of these
acts, naturally turned to them as exhibitions of perfect
goodness, all systems of ethics founded upon innate moral
perceptions must be false. But happily this is not so.
Those who embrace these doctrines do so, because they
are still in that stage, in which men consider it more irre-
ligious to question the infallibility of an Apostle than to
disfigure by any conceivable imputation the character of
the Deity. They esteem it a commendable exercise of
humility to stifle the moral feelings of our nature, and at
last succeed in persuading themselves that their Divinity
would be extremely offended if they hesitate to ascribe to
him the attributes of a fiend." (*H. E. M.* Vol. I. pp. 99,
100.)

The language of Mr Mill in his posthumous *Essays*
is equally strong.

"Even in the Christianity of the Gospels, at least in
its ordinary interpretation, there are some moral difficulties and perversions of so flagrant a character as almost
to outweigh all the beauty, benignity, and moral greatness
which so eminently distinguish the sayings and character
of Christ. The recognition of the highest object of worship
in a Being who could make a hell, and create countless
generations of human beings with the certain foreknowledge
that he was creating them for such a fate. Is there any
moral enormity which might not be justified by imitation
of such a Deity? Is it possible to adore such a one
without a frightful distortion of the standard of right and
wrong? Any other of the outrages to the most ordinary

justice and humanity involved in the common Christian conception of the character of God sinks into insignificance beside this dreadful idealization of wickedness." (pp. 113—4.)

In these passages the real statements of Scripture, the faulty impressions of some imperfect and immature believers, and illusions of the writers themselves, are so strangely blended and confused, as to create a picture most odious and repulsive to every benevolent and pious mind. We are painfully reminded of those "hard speeches" of direct reproach against the Lord of glory, which St Jude predicts as to be spoken by scoffers in the last days. The taunts of the first writer, in which he represents the saved as gloating over the tortures of the lost, though founded on the expressions in Rev. xviii. 20, xix. 2, 3, are alien from the true spirit of those solemn passages, and from the feelings and conscience of all pious men. To believe that God is good and wise in all his ways, and will be seen hereafter to be good and wise, even in the doom of lost souls, when the veil of sense is removed, and we see all things in the light of heaven, is the hardest exercise of Christian faith. Christians succeed in it, however, not by quietly accepting cold, heartless, selfish pride as the character of all the saved, but by a secret conviction that in this aspect of God's dealing with his creatures, there is some mystery, not yet plainly revealed, and such as will hereafter make plain to us what we cannot now understand. The invectives heaped on the history in Numbers, and on the thrice holy name of the God of Israel, are based on a shameless perversion of the facts of the record. The charge to Israel was not to murder an innocent people, but to execute God's own righteous sentence against the most guilty and polluted race existing on the face of the whole earth. And a decree of absolute reprobation, whereby millions were foreappointed to eternal torment, in a way wholly independent of their own guilt and rebellion, so that this rebellion was decreed in the second place, to prepare them for their doom, is a doctrine held by some few, to the great dishonour of God, and injury of their own souls, but always repelled and denounced by the main body of Christian believers, as a hateful perversion and parody of the Divinely revealed warnings of future judgment.

Apart from details, and the hateful and blasphemous inversion of the moral features of the history in the Book of Numbers, of which the sublime beauty and grandeur might well awe even the proudest scoffers into silence and shame, the main force of the objection in these three writers depends on that falsehood, secretly assumed, which it has been the chief object of the previous pages to expose and overthrow. I mean the doctrine that the conflict of good and evil is an arbitrary thing, and that Divine Omnipotence means the power to condense into any single moment of time all those great results of redeeming mercy, which in God's revealed plan are seen to spread over the past millennia of the world's history, and the countless generations of the age to come. It is the false assumption that, because God does not put an end to moral evil, and avert all its fatal consequences from those who despise his commands, and rebel against them, He must be, in some way or another, an accomplice in their crimes, and hatefully and causelessly cruel, should He execute threatened judgment on the disobedient in a life to come. A doctrine, nowhere affirmed in Scripture, and incapable of any proof from sound reason, but derived only from crude, imperfect conceptions of almightiness, that God could any moment save all men and devils if He thought fit so to do; a doctrine which has no surer ground in reason 'than two other assertions plainly false, that God can lie, and that He can create a second God, equal to himself; has blotted out from men's minds the solemn oath of God by the prophet, that He has no pleasure in the death of the sinner, and has caused a dark cloud to settle down over the whole firmament of truth Divinely revealed.

But even when this mischievous and fatal perversion of God's message has been set aside, and we recognize the sincerity and earnestness of the Divine warnings addressed to sinners, to persuade them to forsake the paths of evil, and to guide their feet into the way of peace, a grave difficulty remains in these revealed warnings of judgment to come. Let us inquire, with reverence, what the exact nature of this difficulty is, and whether any light can be thrown upon it, by which the dark cloud may have some bow of promise and hope impressed upon it, though its darkness may not and cannot be wholly removed on this side of the judgment day.

First, then, it is a solemn truth, plainly revealed, that there is a life and a judgment to come. "It is appointed unto men once to die, but after this the judgment." "We must all appear before the judgment seat of Christ." "So then every one shall give account of himself unto God." And in that judgment there is also revealed a great separation. The King will set the sheep on his right hand, and the goats on his left. On both He will pronounce his righteous sentence. "And these shall go away into everlasting punishment, but the righteous into life everlasting." There is an opposite character in the two states that follow, but the same duration, expressed by the same word, which denotes the eternity of God himself. It is true, further, with regard to this great moral contrast, that the word of God, in all ages of the world down to the visions in Patmos, speaks of the ungodly as many and the righteous in God's sight as a little flock, or comparatively few, though their last gathering is also described as "a multitude which no man can number." The words of Christ are most awakening and solemn. "Wide is the gate, and broad is the way, that leadeth to destruction, and many there be which go in thereat; because strait is the gate, and narrow is the way, that leadeth to life, and few there be that find it."

What, then, is the question which must, apart from all the invectives or misrepresentations of unbelievers, weigh on the heart and mind of every thoughtful and devout Christian, when he meditates on the works and ways of his Father in heaven? Does his word set before us a scheme of providence, in which salvation and destruction run side by side for ever, where the lost are many, and the saved comparatively few, where the misery of the lost is as unbroken, intense, and complete as the happiness of the saved; and hopeless damnation and perfect misery, even more widely than bliss and salvation, are the final issue of God's dealings with mankind, and the whole intelligent universe? Is this the consummation, for the speedy fulfilment of which every Christian is called upon to pray and to hope with eager and intense desire? Does a right and orthodox faith in eternal judgment, and the double testimony of Scripture and experience on the past and present abounding of ungodliness, compel us to accept this view of the world to come? Can this faith constitute the glad tidings of great joy, the sum of the everlasting Gospel, which the Son of God came down from heaven to proclaim

to mankind, and of which He has secured the future fulfilment by his life-long humiliation, his bitter agonies and
atoning death ?

To avoid these perplexities, some Christians would
advise us to stifle all thought, and forbear all inquiry into
the ways of God. But that remedy is worse than the
disease. For the careless worldling the only answer should
be that of our Lord himself—Strive to enter in at the
strait gate. But the children of God must not borrow
from the doctrine of annihilation, and strive to extinguish
the noblest faculties and instincts of a spiritual being.
They must seek to understand the character, mind, and
will of their Father, and to read his love and wisdom in
all his ways. It is their bounden duty to seek for this
light, so far as it is attainable, and to suffer no cloud to
rest on their view of his love, holiness, and wisdom, which
patient thought and careful study of his word can remove;
but to wait with patience for fuller light, whenever clouds
and darkness, which they are unable to pierce, still surround the ways of the Most High.

The first main step towards the removal of that sore
moral perplexity, which seems inseparable from the view
of redemption usual among Christian Divines, is the
doctrine I have unfolded in the Four Prophetic Empires,
and the Outlines of unfulfilled prophecy, and which has
since then been accepted by many other students of Scripture, and embodied in their works. The church of the
first-born, the mystic bride of Christ, does not sum up and
exhaust all the fruits of redeeming love. In the glory of
that Church the truth of electing grace will be manifested
for ever. But a wider truth of redeeming grace will also
be seen in successive generations of redeemed men, the
subjects of Christ's kingdom, over whom He will reign

with his Church in that new earth, where righteousness is
to dwell for ever. To these generations, and the increase
of the saved, there is no limit revealed. The absolute
infinity of the Divine nature will thus have a fit theatre
for its display, and a kind of passive image and reflection,
in this capacity of man's nature for multiplication and
increase, and successive and wider unfoldings of the Divine
goodness. Of the increase of Christ's kingdom there shall
be no end. Thus the number of the elect church may be
far less than of the souls that are condemned in the judgment, but the number of the saved who walk in the light
of the celestial city may be vastly greater, and continually
increase world without end.

The second truth, which may help to remove the dark
cloud resting on the Divine character in the popular creed
of Christians, is the view of omnipotence, unfolded in the
earlier part of this work. God's warnings and threatenings
are not arbitrary and capricious things, the result of naked
sovereignty alone. The conflict of Divine goodness with
the power of evil is no mere pretence or empty show,
which might cease any moment by a bare act of God's
sovereign will. The solemn oath of the Most High must
be received in its unforced and natural meaning, and not
made void by the groundless assertion, that of course God
could save all men and devils any moment, and only for-
bears to do so for some wise reason. "As I live, saith the
Lord, I have no pleasure in the death of the sinner, but
rather that he should be converted and live. Turn ye,
turn ye, for why will ye die, O house of Israel? For I
have no pleasure in the death of him that dieth; wherefore
turn yourselves and live." The ruin of those who perish
must thus be ascribed wholly to their own sin, and not in
part or wholly to a denial, on God's part, of some grace,

which might easily have been given. And thus, in the great day of account, God will be justified in his sayings, and be clear when He stands in judgment. The contrast, taught by St James, will come out clearly into view in the face of the whole universe, that God cannot be tempted of evil, and tempteth no man, that every good and perfect gift is from the Father of lights, and that all sin and evil is from the creature alone. Men may strive, in their unbelief and perverseness, to cast the blame of their own sins upon the Creator. But all such vain excuses will cease, and their hard speeches be silenced, when He who wept tears of sorrow over Jerusalem, and shed drops of blood in his agony in the garden, shall be seen upon the throne of his glory, the appointed Judge of all mankind.

But there is a further truth, which, I believe, may be learned from a strict comparison of all the statements of Scripture with reference to the future punishment of the unsaved, and is a further help for seeing the real harmony between this solemn part of the Divine message, and the perfect wisdom and goodness of the Most High. It is a truth, not lying on the surface of the harvest field of Scripture, but beneath its surface, as treasures are hid in the mine. The mines of a country, however, are no less really a part of its riches, than its oaks and cedars, its vineyards, olive yards, and cornfields. The faith and reverence of the Christian are due, not only to what he reads in the express words of Scripture, but to every thing which, when we seek Divine wisdom as silver, and search for it as for hid treasure, is found hidden in this blessed field, and may be proved thereby.

I will now endeavour to unfold, in some distinct propositions, what I believe to be the real teaching of Scrip-

ture, negatively and positively, on this solemn subject of
the Second Death and Eternal Judgment.

I. First, the Second Death is not the reign of Satan in
a kingdom of his own, in which he reigns over those whom
he has deceived, and actively torments them for ever.

This view has been very often held and set forth in popular
appeals to the fears of men with regard to the coming judgment. It is found, not seldom, in the pages of Christian
Divines. Of the two authors by whom my own view, when
first published ten years ago, was vehemently assailed, while
one agrees with me in rejecting it, the other has maintained it, as if it were an integral part of the orthodox
creed upon future punishment. But of all men's vain
additions to and corruptions of Scripture doctrine, none is
more groundless than this, or more wholly opposed to the
real teaching of the word of God. We read in St John
the great end of our Lord's advent and work. "For this
purpose was the Son of God manifested, that he might
destroy the works of the devil." The fire, to which the
ungodly are sentenced, is said to have been "prepared for
the devil and his angels." Before their judgment that
solemn announcement is made, "And the devil that deceived them was cast into the lake of fire and brimstone,
and shall be tormented day and night for ever and ever."
The foremost and chief in guilt will then be foremost and
deepest in punishment. He who is "king over all the children of pride" will be crushed, beyond all the proud, under
the heaviest strokes of Divine judgment. The head of
the serpent will be bruised under the feet of the Seed of
the Woman, the destined Redeemer of mankind.

No trace of any permitted reign of this Prince of darkness can be found, when once death and hell have been cast
into the lake of fire. Death is the last enemy to be

destroyed. All others, Satan included, must therefore, in their power of active rebellion, have been destroyed, before death and hell are cast into that lake of fire. "Whosoever exalteth himself shall be abased." This is the great, unalterable law of God's moral government. And hence this Lucifer, son of the morning, who once exalted himself the highest in blasphemous pride, as the rival and adversary of God, will then be lowest in shame among those vanquished enemies, the appointed footstool of the lowly Man of sorrows, who is also the "King of kings and Lord of lords."

An opposite assertion has been made, that "Satan will still reign supreme in the realms of perdition, and possess a greater amount of mingled malice and power, to render miserable those who died in this world as his subjects and slaves." And it is said further to be needless to quote any passages from the Bible in proof of this doctrine. Its wide acceptance is a sufficient proof without one grain of Scripture evidence, since the writer had met with no believer in future punishment, who ever doubted, much less denied it.

In the place of evidence which Scripture does not supply, but the reverse, a moral argument for this view has been proposed. "It would be strange if there should be less enmity, ferocity, and fighting, than prevail amongst the most depraved of wicked men in this world. This must imply that the ungodly will be much better characters hereafter than on earth. The just punishment of Satan and his angels has not in the least improved them, though they have been tormented without a moment's intermission for six thousand years."

This last statement has no warrant in God's word, but is rather directly opposed to it. Satan is there called the God of this world, exercising a large permitted power through Divine forbearance, appearing in heavenly places among the sons of God, and looking forward with dread to a time of judgment still to come. The dæmons in the Gospel, also, utter the cry, Art thou come hither to torment us before the time? There is thus the widest contrast between the present time of Satan's permitted activity and reign, and the future season of his punishment, when all his power to tempt or accuse the brethren, or to reign over evil men, will have ceased for ever. It is not strange, but natural and certain, that sinners should have less freedom for active wickedness under the fiery anger of God than in the time of his forbearance and longsuffering. Nothing can be more monstrous than the notion that, under the holy eye and righteous hand of the Supreme Judge, they both can and will rebel more freely and fiercely than ever before. Such a prison, in which criminals should be allowed to cultivate their own wicked habits and practices to the uttermost, would be a foul reproach to any earthly government. How great, then, must be the evil of bringing this charge, without the least grain of Scripture evidence, nay, in the teeth of its express statements, against the government of the Righteous and Eternal King!

Satan, in the judgment, is not loosed but bound, and not only bound, but cast into the lake of fire. The language may be figurative. But the figures are those which most entirely exclude the freedom to tempt, or the power to tyrannise any longer over those who are the partners of his doom. The object of our Lord's mission will then be fulfilled. The works of Satan will be destroyed. The deceiver can tempt no longer, and the Prince of the power of the air can rule no more. The height of his proud and aspiring claims will only measure the depth of his utter humiliation and punishment.

II. Again, the Last Judgment and the Second Death are one main part in a wise, holy, and perfect work of the God of love.

At the close of the law we have this striking proclamation of God's name—"He is the Rock, his work is perfect; all his ways are judgment; a God of truth and without iniquity, just and right is he."

The work of God is perfect. There is no flaw, error, or mistake, in his scheme of universal providence. On the side of the creature there is a vast and awful amount of sin, folly, and perverseness. But in that dominion of God, whereby He overcomes evil, there is no defect either of wisdom or goodness. Though "clouds and darkness are round about him," yet "justice and judgment are the habitation of his throne."

When the prophet was told to go down to the potter's house, "the vessel he made of clay was marred in the hands of the potter, and he made it again another vessel, as it seemed good to the potter to make it." (Jer. xviii. 4.) But the scheme of providence is one mighty whole. Once begun, it can never be reversed, or begun anew. One single flaw, in this case, would be irreparable, and could never be cured. One unjust or unwise act of the God of Providence, like one sin in the spotless and perfect obedience of Christ, would mar the perfection, and change the character, of the whole work. Creation, Providence, Redemption, would be reduced to one gigantic and irretrievable failure. But this can never be. "His work is perfect." The forbearance towards evil, while it lasts, and seems even to triumph, is a perfect forbearance, meted out by infinite wisdom and grace. The victory

over evil, when that forbearance is ended, must be a
perfect victory. The issues of judgment, however solemn,
must be such that the All-wise, whose understanding is
unsearchable, the All-good, whose tender mercies are over
all his works, can not only acquiesce in them, but even
rejoice in them, with a deep complacency of divine love.
"The glory of the Lord shall endure for ever, the Lord
shall rejoice in his works." His delight will be evermore
to exercise " loving-kindness, judgment, and righteousness
in the earth."

Now this revealed perfection of the whole work of
God, when we reflect on it calmly, must throw a steady
light on this mysterious and solemn subject of the Second
Death. The first death is God's last and greatest enemy.
It may be borne with for a time, but its continuance
would be a fatal barrier to the dominion and glory of the
Most High. " God is not the God of the dead, but of the
living." And hence that indignant sentence—"O death,
I will be thy plagues ; O grave, I will be thy destruction."
But the second death proceeds directly from the appointment of the Supreme Judge, who is perfect both in
wisdom and goodness. However terrible and solemn, it is
his Divine remedy for all that is most fearful and appal-
ling in the actual or possible evil of a fallen and rebellious
universe. The God of love and holiness can and will
acquiesce in it, as one main element in his foreordained
counsel of wisdom and goodness. The attempt to deepen
its terrors by heaping up all kinds of moral and spiritual
horrors, the unchecked ravings of fiendish malice, the
blasphemous utterances of raging despair, and to see in
it the stereotyped continuation of rebellion, hatred and
blasphemy for ever, is to reverse and deny the revealed
object and aim of the work of Christ. "For this purpose

was the Son of God manifested, that he might destroy the works of the devil." The grand purpose of the judgment which He will execute can never be to stereotype and eternize active rebellion against God, but to abolish it for evermore.

The Second Death, therefore, however solemn, completes a work of the only wise God, which is perfect, and cannot be improved. It crowns the victory of his perfect goodness over the worst malignity and the most inveterate forms of evil.

III. The doom of the lost, we are further taught, will be the object of acquiescence and holy contemplation on the part of all the unfallen and the redeemed.

With those views of hell torment which have been widely current in the church, to hide it from the thoughts must be almost essential to happiness, in hearts not wholly dead to feelings of compassion. The bliss of heaven must then be conceived to depend very mainly on the removal of its inhabitants far away from sights and sounds so unutterably mournful. Such, however, is not the revealed description of saints and angels in the kingdom of God. Their happiness is not made to depend either on their ignorance or their forgetfulness of the doom of the lost. On the contrary, this is placed among the objects of their ceaseless contemplation. That punishment is said to be " in the presence of the holy angels, and in the presence of the Lamb."

These descriptions, again, are made the ground, by unbelievers, of the severest and keenest invectives against the horrible selfishness which the orthodox creed imputes to all the redeemed. One passage has been given, where this charge is made in language of the most bitter sarcasm.

Yet the apostle, on whose descriptions of coming judgment these charges are founded, is the same to whom we owe those sublime definitions of true piety: "God is love, and he that dwelleth in love dwelleth in God, and God in him." "If a man say, I love God, and hateth his brother, he is a liar. For he that loveth not his brother, whom he hath seen, how can he love God, whom he hath not seen?"

The texts, then, on which these invectives have been founded, teach really an opposite lesson. The acquiescence described will not be that of stern, fierce, revengeful, unloving hearts, but of the spirits of just men made perfect, dwelling in the light of the pure, all-perfect goodness, and baptized by the Spirit into fullest sympathy with the tears, compassion, and agonies of the Son of God. That doom, however solemn, can hardly be one of unmingled horror and darkness, much less of abounding and eternal blasphemy, which is the object of complacency and holy adoration to saints and angels, free from all taint of mere selfishness, and moulded into the full and perfect resemblance of the Divine love.

IV. Fourthly, on the day of judgment the honour due even to the wicked, as God's creatures, and gifted by Him with high and noble powers, will, in some way or other, be still recognized by the righteous Judge.

The law of God is the reflection of his own righteousness. And the life of man is there fenced by this threatening;—"Whoso sheddeth man's blood, by man shall his blood be shed; for in the image of God made he man." Many murdered persons have been themselves most degraded and vile. Yet the sacredness of man's life is measured, not by the debasement sin has caused, but by God's own creative ordinance. "In the image of God made he man."

This principle, the voice of God's own truth and wisdom, must therefore apply to his own acts of righteous judgment. Even when He punishes guilty rebels, He does not cease to honour in them the workmanship of his own hands. And hence this reason is assigned for the mitigation or suspense of his temporal judgments: "for the spirit would fail before me, and *the souls which I have made.*"

Again, in the law we find this limit assigned to the judge, when a wicked man was to be punished for his transgressions : "Forty stripes he may give him, and not exceed : lest, if he should exceed, and beat him above these with many stripes, then thy brother should seem vile unto thee."

Here a double lesson is taught. The wickedness which deserves and requires stripes is not to destroy the sense of brotherhood. Even while punished, the wicked man is called a brother still. And the punishment must be so measured, that his due honour as a brother may not perish. He who gave this law is the same in whose heart, as the Son of man, it was afterwards written, and who will pronounce the final sentence on the ungodly. The stripes, few or many, in the great day of account, will be fixed by his sentence alone. Luke xii. 45—48. The doom He will pronounce, having for its measure the deep malignity of sin, may be unutterably severe. But this law is a pledge and assurance that the Righteous Judge will still remember the honour of all men as God's creatures, made at first in his image, and that brotherhood which, through the incarnation, has linked Him so closely with even the most guilty and rebellious of mankind.

V. Once more, the last judgment is the work of

B.   P

God's mercy as well as of his judicial righteousness. This is plainly taught us in those striking and impressive words of the Psalmist—"Also unto thee, O Lord, belongeth mercy; for thou renderest to every man according to his work."

In the judgment of the righteous it is easy to see and feel the truth of this inspired message of God. The works rewarded are the fruits of the Spirit, and can flow from redeeming mercy alone. Hence the reward, as in the baptismal prayer of our church, must be traced back to its true fountain head of Divine mercy and love.

But when we seek to apply the words, in their wider range, to every man, to the lost as well as the saved, the message is deeper and more mysterious. Can it be true, even of the souls that perish, that there is mercy in that sentence, which dooms them to the lake of fire? The deep thought, which Plato dimly apprehended by the light of nature, seems here to receive a direct sanction from the Spirit of God. Punishment is set before us in the light of a Divine medicine for the diseases of the soul. Compared with that most awful of curses, that evil should be left to work out fully its own terrible issues in the darkness of utter banishment from the Divine presence, even the justice of God, however severe, is medicinal to guilty sinners. Their doom is awful, but a world abandoned to the reign of unrestrained and triumphant wickedness would be still more awful. The abyss or bottomless pit, boundless in its breadth and depth, and insatiable in its craving, is to be destroyed and abolished by the power of the Redeemer. The revealed scene of judgment is not a sea, an ocean or abyss, but simply a lake of fire. It is mercy to the wicked to deny them the fatal power of adding sin to sin. It is mercy to keep them from the power of tormenting each other, by the free indulgence of their own sinful and hateful passions. It is mercy to force them back, even though captive and in chains, to the presence of that infinite goodness, from which their own rebellious hearts would lead them farther and farther away, till they should lose themselves deeper and deeper in delusion and darkness for ever.

VI. Again, the Second Death is the sequel of a resurrection, but a resurrection to "shame and everlasting contempt." Dan. xii. 2. It thus involves in its very nature contrasted elements. For resurrection is a work of redemption, a triumph over death, and a fruit of the atoning work of the world's Redeemer. But a resurrection to shame and contempt must also be a perpetual manifestation of the creature's moral emptiness, in contrast to the immutable and glorious perfection of Him who is the Only Wise, and the Only Good.

It obscures the Gospel, and distorts our view of the whole course of Providence, when we ascribe a result so awful to some capricious, unaccountable withholding of Divine grace. This would surely imply some great defect either of wisdom or goodness in the Almighty, and his deliberate preference of the destruction of multitudes of sinners to their salvation. An oath of the Most High has been sworn, to shield his name from this dark suspicion of unbelieving hearts, which have never fathomed the sinfulness of sin, or the stubbornness of evil. And even in spite of God's solemn protest, the falsehood has often entwined itself with the most sacred truths and mysteries of the Gospel. But when we refer this solemn fact to the essential contrast between the Only Good and the creatures of his hand, we may see how redemption turns what might else appear like an incurable triumph of evil into the crown and seal of a perfect victory of redeeming love. It may be this continual spectacle of what the creature is in itself, which alone maintains the whole universe of unfallen and ransomed creatures in its only true and safe position of entire dependence on the great Fountain of life and love.

The Israelites, in entering the land of promise, were warned of a great moral danger, that their heart might be lifted up when once their victory was accomplished, and they might forget the Lord their God. And when the work of redemption is complete in countless myriads of ransomed souls, and successive generations of the righteous, so that no trace of sin, corruption, or mortality remains in the dwellers on the new earth, or in the heavenly city, how easily might pride creep in once more, and a second and more fatal apostasy ensue; if the lessons of the past, fading ever into the far distance of by-gone years, were not renewed and deepened by the present spectacle of those in whom there is an everlasting memorial of the past reign of evil, and of the creature's self-emptiness and utter shame! Their solemn doom, though no result of the choice of the Most High, whose love has displayed itself to the utmost in solemn warnings to deter sinners from the path of ruin, may yet be the object of his deep and holy acquiescence; because in this way alone a ransomed universe can be upheld for ever in a blessedness based on perfect humility, and capable on that very account of enlarging and unfolding itself, without risk of fresh apostasy, for evermore. And thus it may be that, through the resurrection to judgment and shame, the bulwarks will be completed of that celestial city, whose walls are Salvation, and her gates Praise.

CHAPTER XIV.

ON ETERNAL JUDGMENT, CONCLUDED.

THE New Testament throws further and perhaps still clearer light on this solemn truth of eternal punishment, when we look below the surface, and strive to combine the indirect with the direct and open lessons which its sacred messages convey.

I. Every created being may be viewed in two different aspects, personal and federal, or what it is of itself, and its character as part of a greater whole. This warp and woof runs through the whole of Scripture, and occasions a frequent antithesis in its statements of Divine truth. Thus in "Adam all die," and still "the soul that sinneth, it shall die." In Christ "all shall be made alive," and still it is to those who by patient continuance in well doing seek for glory, honour, and immortality, that God will render eternal life. The charge to the Galatians, "Bear ye one another's burdens, and so fulfil the law of Christ," is followed at once by an opposite statement, as the attendant moral caution, "For every one shall bear his own burden." St Paul says to the Corinthians, "He that planteth and he that watereth are one," and then adds at once,—"Every man shall receive his reward according to his own labour."

The same contrast, wherever selfishness is not complete, is found by experience in the elements which constitute human happiness and misery, joy and sorrow. In part they are purely and simply personal, but in part they arise from sympathy with the joys or sorrows of others, or from the contemplation of truths not personal, but objective and universal. Thus the wounded soldier or sailor may often almost forget his wounds in his deep delight in his commander's triumph, or the overthrow of his country's enemy. There are many cases in which the sense of pain is almost lost, from the presence of some absorbing object of thought, or tidings of the happiness and honour of those who are deeply beloved. The Christian, whatever his personal peace or comfort, may have deep sorrow from the sight of abounding sin, and the thought of a Saviour dishonoured, or of perishing souls; and times of bereavement have their anguish lightened by faith in the increased happiness of the friends or kindred whom death has removed.

Thus all happiness is of two kinds, personal or federal. The first results from experiences which are strictly and properly our own. The other has a wider range, and depends on our power to pass in thought out of ourselves, to sympathize with the feelings and joys of others, to dwell on the interests of our family, our church, or our nation, and grieve or rejoice in all that affects their welfare; or to rise above merely personal sensations, and contemplate external, objective, and eternal truth.

Now all the statements of Scripture with respect to the future doom, in judgment, of the righteous and the wicked, have direct reference to personal conduct and personal retribution. The federal aspect, in these passages, does not appear. The statements are of this kind:

" Every man shall bear his own burden "; " Whatsoever a man soweth, that shall he reap"; " Every one shall receive his reward according to his own labour "; " My reward is with me, to give every man according as his work shall be"; " He that soweth sparingly shall reap sparingly, and he that soweth bountifully shall reap also bountifully "; " The Son of man shall come in the glory of his Father, and then shall he render to every man according to his works"; "He called his servants, that he might know how much every man had gained by trading".

The result of this personal judgment, by the repeated testimony of many Scriptures, is a final contrast, an eternal separation, depending on the use or abuse of the probation in this mortal life. The earnest appeals to men to repent and turn to God derive the main part of their force from this all-pervading truth, often expressed, and everywhere implied, in their large variety of warnings, threatenings, promises, and earnest and affectionate appeals to the hearts of men.

But this truth, however solemn, and however inwrought into the doctrine of man's personal responsibility, cannot exclude a further truth, namely, the federal relation of all mankind to the Creator of the universe, and to Christ, the Head of every man, the Saviour of the world, who gave himself a ransom for all men. One of these truths is no less deeply inwrought into the texture of God's word than the other. It must reveal its reality and its power, in some way or other, amidst all the solemn and tremendous realities of the coming judgment.

II. Secondly, the Second Death is a work of the God of truth, by which pride and falsehood are to be abolished out of the moral universe.

The New Testament opens with the history of the

conflict of the tempter, the king of pride, with the meek
and lowly Redeemer. And the result of this conflict is
embodied in that maxim, so often repeated, "Whosoever
exalteth himself shall be abased; but he that humbleth
himself shall be exalted."

This great maxim will receive an endless variety of illus-
trations. But the first and chief is the contrasted doom of
the proud tempter and of the lowly Man of sorrows. The
Son of God, because He stooped so low, is crowned with
eternal and infinite glory. The Adversary, the proud Son
of the morning, because he said in his heart, I will be like
the Most High, will suffer perpetual shame, and the vengeance of eternal fire. That fire, prepared for the devil
and his angels, must be the destruction of guilty pride,
when it has become in a manner consubstantiate with the
spirit, and can be overcome in no gentler way than by
these ever-during strokes of Divine judgment. "Them that
walk in pride he is able to abase." The created being itself
will not fail. It is a gift of God without repentance, and
is secretly upheld by his mighty hand. But that stubbornness of pride, which may be no longer separable along
with the sinful flesh, as it was with sinful men in their
day of grace, will encounter something firmer than itself,
the inflexible holiness of the God of judgment. Proud
imaginations, the high things that exalt themselves against
the knowledge of Christ, which stumble at his warnings,
and refuse to see the depth of grace in his sufferings, are
idols of the heart. And these idols God will utterly
abolish. The last great day will be "against everything
that is high and lifted up, and it shall be brought low."
The rebellious creature must be taught, in spite of itself,
to take its true and right place at the footstool of triumphant holiness. "Lord, when thy hand is lifted up, they

will not see; but they shall see, and be ashamed." The twin reign of falsehood and of pride must cease, under the searching, humbling presence of the God of truth and holiness, which is and must be a consuming fire, to abolish every form of delusion and rebellious pride.

III. Thirdly, the Second Death is a work of the God of love, wherein He displays his holy anger against every sinner, whose heart and life have been marked by utter selfishness, and the entire absence of genuine love to God and men.

The revealed ground of the condemning sentence is given by our Lord in these words: "Inasmuch as ye did it not to one of the least of these, ye did it not unto me." The absence of the works and fruits of love is here made the ground and cause of their fearful doom. The excellency of true and genuine love is taught by the severity of the sentence, for which the want of love is the sole cause assigned by the Supreme Judge.

The Judge, then, who pronounces the sentence, must be perfect in love, and in love even to those on whom the sentence falls. The Holy One cannot be a sharer in the sin which He visits on these his creatures with such severe and righteous condemnation. The Second Death, then, implies the highest honour given to love as the crowning grace, the very image of the Divine perfection; and also the exercise of such love by the Judge himself, even towards those on whom He denounces a doom so terrible for the guilt and crime of a selfish and unloving heart.

It may be a deep mystery how Divine love can possibly reveal itself at all, where Divine righteousness will be displayed in a sentence of everlasting punishment and shame. But the things which are hard or impossible with men are possible with God. If righteousness and grace coexist for ever in the infinite perfection of the Most High, their exercise may coexist for ever, even in his dealings with those whose rejection of offered grace involves the solemn necessity that this righteousness should assume the form of irreversible and ever-during punishment. Every stroke of the Avenger will be a testimony to God's anger against hatred and selfishness, and his delight in pure, genuine, and perfect love.

IV. Fourthly, the Resurrection to Judgment, like the Resurrection of Life, is one part of the redeeming work of Christ.

The two main issues of judgment, however great their contrast, have one feature common to both. They follow a resurrection. Hence the Apostle unites them in one common statement, before he marks the contrast between "them that are Christ's," and all others. "For since by man came death, by man came also the resurrection of the dead. For as in Adam all die, even so in Christ shall all be made alive."

The first death in every case has come through the sin of Adam. The life-restoring resurrection is to come in every case through the power and work of the Second Adam, the Lord from heaven. The judgment on the lost is based on a present work of the Redeemer, in which they share with the saved, and on a victory over death, wrought by Christ, and depending on the power of his atoning sacrifice and resurrection from the dead. Their bodies are restored from the earlier dominion of the grave, and the dominion of death, so far, is wholly abolished.

Now what is implied in this truth, so plainly and fully revealed? The contrast of state, due to the contrast of faith and unbelief, of personal repentance or perseverance in rebellion, during the time of probation, is to abide and endure. The resurrection of the unjust seems to me a plain and insurmountable argument against the doctrine of annihilation, as the doom of the disobedient. The result which follows directly from the sin of the first Adam, is to be reversed and repealed through the grace and power of the second Adam, the Lord from heaven. For all mankind there has been a federal ruin, and thus "in Adam all die." For all mankind, so far as the death of the body is concerned, there is a federal recovery from that ruin, and thus "in Christ shall all be made alive." The opposite results of personal character are to remain and endure. But common results of the Redeemer's work, who is the Head of every man, are to abide and endure also. The lesson of the Divine law will thus be renewed on a magnified scale and in a deeply mysterious form. The wicked man, who is worthy of stripes, few or many, will be beaten by the sentence of the righteous Judge. But at the same time his brotherhood with that Judge will be revealed for ever by the resurrection which precedes the work of judgment.

In the first death the dissolution of the body, and its corruption, was only the type, sign, and parable of the deeper curse resting on the spirit, when it had wandered or was driven away from the presence of Him who is Light and Love. And when the dead are raised by the power of Christ, this correspondence cannot wholly cease. When death and hell are cast into the lake of fire, the souls, even of the lost, can remain no longer under the curse of utter vanity. They will glorify their Maker, even amidst the fires of penal judgment. To glorify God is the great end, for which every creature was made. If the dealings of God with any creature were such as to justify a charge of unnatural cruelty or excessive and needless severity, God could not possibly be glorified thereby, but rather the

Divine glory would be obscured, deeply clouded, or blotted out and wholly destroyed. To glorify God, through shame and punishment, compared with the bliss of the redeemed and holy, must be an infinite and irreparable loss. But to glorify Him in any way, however solemn and mournful, when contrasted with the reign of that death which is God's enemy, and the curse of eternal vanity, darkness, and corruption, may be, even to the souls of the lost, a real, and perhaps even in some respects, an infinite gain.

V. The love of Christ, we are told by the Apostle, has a breadth and length and depth and height, that passeth knowledge. Its breadth may be seen in the multitude of its objects, extending to angels and men, and countless multitudes in successive generations. Its length is shewn in its endurance through eternal ages. Its height is revealed in the glory of the Church of the firstborn, and of the risen saints, who are exalted to share in the Redeemer's kingdom and throne. Its depth has been revealed, once for all, in his own agony and death, when He endured the curse, and went down to darkness and the lowest deep for man's redemption. But is the manifestation of this dimension of that Divine attribute wholly to cease? Must not rather the infinite depth, as well as height of His love, be manifested for ever? This is surely the view most consistent with the revealed statement of the fourfold vastness of that Divine and all-perfect love.

And in whom can this depth of the love of Christ be displayed for ever? Must it not be in the guilty and condemned, who are said to be raised only to shame and everlasting contempt? Towards these the love of God, if displayed at all, must assume its most strange, perplexing, and mysterious form. But since it has a depth that passeth knowledge, our small ability, in the present life,

to understand or imagine the mode of its exercise cannot
exclude either its possibility or its actual reality. May it
not be shown in the perpetual yearnings of a deep and
true compassion ? When spirits, once stubborn and rebellious, have been crushed under the fire of Divine wrath,
and they are conscious that their persevering rebellion
has lost them a glory once within their reach, which they
were lovingly intreated to embrace, but never to be regained,
and brought them under a sentence never to be repealed,
the depth of a love which can stoop infinitely low, and
encompass them even there with Divine compassion, may
pierce through their conscience, and pervade their whole
being, even amidst their still abiding consciousness of
deepest loss and eternal shame. Like Israel, self-destroyed,
their only hope of any form or share of relief and consola-
tion must be in a love that passeth human knowledge,
and can visit them even in the lowest gulf of a misery
otherwise without hope of cure or mitigation. The truth
of God seems to give a most solemn assurance that the
penal sentence shall never be reversed. The depth of a
love that passeth knowledge gives an equal assurance, that
their doom shall not be, however terrible and mournful,
one of unmitigated misery, but such that, even here, the
glory of the Divine goodness, and those tender mercies of
God which are over all his works, shall be revealed for
evermore.

The Apostle tells us further of the living God, that
He is "the Saviour of all men, specially of them that
believe." That holy and blessed name of Saviour is signally and specially revealed in the future glory and bliss
of believers alone. But still He is also the Saviour of all
men. Can this refer to temporal blessings merely, that will
soon cease, and be followed by total, absolute destruction

and ruin? Can it be fulfilled in conditional benefits made
wholly fruitless, and turned into an abiding curse through
the perverseness of sinners? How can this agree with
our Lord's reasoning on the title, the God of Abraham,
Isaac and Jacob? Such a name, He distinctly tells us,
requires no transient, but an enduring character and relation. And it would seem that in this other Divine title
the same rule of sacred reason must apply.

Unbelievers are not saved from judgment, from the
condemning sentence of their Judge, from righteous punishment, and the second death, from shame and everlasting
contempt, from the fire that is not quenched. These
warnings are sealed by the lips of Him whose name is the
Truth; and I see not how either universalism or annihilation can be held without making void, wholly or partly,
his threatenings, and contradicting the true sayings of
God. But these threatenings, however deeply true, are not
necessarily the whole truth. This title of God must surely
imply some further truth, not only consistent with, but
needful to complete, the Divine veracity. Unbelievers
are included among all men, of whom it is expressly declared that in some sense or other, God, the living God is
the Saviour. They will be saved from temporal death and
bodily corruption, "for as in Adam all die, even so in
Christ shall all be made alive." They will be saved from
that first death, in which the creature is self-ruined, and
God is not glorified at all, but for ever blasphemed. They
will be saved from the curse of hopeless vanity, in which
the great end of their creation remains wholly unfulfilled.
They will be saved from that abyss, unsearchable in its
depth and unfathomable in its darkness, when death and
the abyss are cast into the lake of fire. Will they not be
saved from that utter unmingled, hopeless misery, in

which no ray of comfort or relief of any kind breaks in upon a dreary solitude of everlasting despair? Will they not be saved, in some strange and mysterious, but real sense, when their irremovable sorrow finds beneath it a still lower depth of Divine compassion, and the sinful creature, in its most forlorn estate, and in its utter shame, encounters the amazing vision of tender, condescending and infinite love?

VI. This great and solemn truth may be viewed, further, in its relation to the clearly revealed moral attributes and perfections of the Most High.

Every child of man is related to God under three distinct characters of the Divine goodness. The first is the simple bounty of the Creator. The second is the equity of the Moral Governor of the world. The third is the mercy and compassion of God the Redeemer.

The Lord is good to every man, and his tender mercies are over all his works. He giveth to all men life and breath and all things. He giveth food to all flesh. He sendeth rain from heaven and fruitful seasons, filling the hearts of men with food and gladness. He is also the God who loveth righteousness and hateth iniquity, who resisteth the proud, and giveth grace to the humble. He is of purer eyes than to behold evil. He is also a God of compassion and grace. He reclaims the lost, restores the wanderer, welcomes the returning prodigal, and visits with tenderest compassion those who have erred and gone astray.

The second character of God is that on which the issues of judgment depend. All men are parted thus into two classes, according to their moral character as known to God, and their use or abuse of proffered grace in the day of their probation. Personal righteousness or unrighteousness is the revealed ground of that predicted eternal contrast and separation.

But the contrast between the obedient and the disobedient, the faithful and unbelieving, in their relation to God as the righteous Judge, cannot set aside their common relation to Him, as the bountiful Creator of all men, and the God of grace towards all who are sunk in guilt or misery. The threefold cord of Divine truth and holiness cannot be broken. The gifts and calling of God are without repentance. The love of the all-wise Creator to all his creatures was brightly displayed in the very fact of their creation. It may be veiled for a time through the dark unfoldings of moral evil and iniquity; but it surely cannot be annihilated, and wholly reversed and blotted out for ever. His judgments, when most awful, must still remain in harmony with his own declaration by the prophet—" I will not contend for ever, neither will I be always wroth ; for the spirit should fail before me, and the souls which I have made." There is a sense in which God will contend for ever, and be always wroth. There is a sense, also, in which He will not so do, lest the effect should be mere annihilation of the noblest works of his own hands. And again, the link between sorrow and misery, however caused and wherever found, and the Divine compassion, must abide and endure. " God so loved the world, that he gave his only begotten Son," to be the propitiation for their sins. The Lamb of God taketh away the sin of the world. When He stooped from his throne, and took on Him our flesh, He became the brother and the head of every man. The law, " Thou shalt love thy neighbour as thyself," was written and engraven in his heart. No depth in the perverseness of evil, no certainty of inexorable righteousness, when the King of heaven sits on the throne of judgment, can ever contract this revealed mercy of the Father and the Son within narrower bounds. Sinners, to whom the Son of God was given, for whom He bore the cross, and died accursed, over whom He wept tears of pity, and towards whom there have been patient yearnings of God's infinite compassion, and of his Divine long-suffering, not willing that any should perish, but that all should come to repentance, can surely never cease, even under the strokes of judgment, and in their depth of utter shame, to be encircled evermore by the infinite compassions of that holy and perfect Being whose very name and nature is Love.

Here, then, let us pause with reverence, and adore. May the All-wise and the All-holy teach us the spirit of the poor and the contrite, who tremble at his word, and who fear Him of whom it is solemnly proclaimed, by the Lord of glory, that He is able to destroy both body and soul in hell. But may He give us further the spirit of undoubting and unwavering faith in his perfect goodness. May we believe firmly, though clouds and darkness are round about Him, and chiefly in the exercise of his revealed judgments on the unholy, the disobedient, and the profane, that those grand and glorious words of his Divine law shall be confirmed and ratified for ever— "He is the Rock, his work is perfect, all his ways are judgment; a God of truth and without iniquity, just and right is He!"

Cambridge:
PRINTED BY C. J. CLAY, M.A.
AT THE UNIVERSITY PRESS.

www.ingramcontent.com/pod-product-compliance
Lightning Source LLC
Chambersburg PA
CBHW030759020726
47499CB00006B/1696